PERFUME
The Alchemy of Scent

Jean-Claude Ellena

PERFUMER AT HERMÈS

Translated by John Crisp

Arcade Publishing
New York

To Susannah

Arcade Publishing books may be purchased in bulk at special discounts for sales promotion, corporate gifts, fund-raising, or educational purposes. Special editions can also be created to specifications. For details, contact the Special Sales Department, Arcade Publishing, 307 West 36th Street, 11th Floor, New York, NY 10018 or arcade@skyhorsepublishing.com.

Arcade Publishing® is a registered trademark of Skyhorse Publishing, Inc.®, a Delaware corporation.

Visit our website at www.arcadepub.com.

10 9 8 7

Library of Congress Cataloging-in-Publication Data is available on file.

ISBN: 978-1-62872-696-1
Ebook ISBN: 978-1-62872-170-6

Printed in the United States of America

CONTENTS

Introduction. v

CHAPTER I: Birth of Modern Perfumery 1

CHAPTER II: The Nose and Odor 11
I. The Sense of Smell • II. The Olfactory System • III. Odor

CHAPTER III: Materials and Substances 19
I. Materials of Natural Origin • II. Techniques for Obtaining
Materials • III. Synthetic Materials • IV. Analysis Techniques
• V. Substances • VI. Formulation Methods

CHAPTER IV: Learning the Trade 35
I. Odor Classifications • II. Memorizing the Collection •
III. Type of Olfactory Field

CHAPTER V: The Trade 43
I. From Know-how to Science • II. Finding a Pretext •
III. Olfactory Illusions • IV. Writing Down a Perfume •
V. A Curious Mind • VI. A Creative Mind • VII. Perseverance,
Certainty, Doubt • VIII. Rejecting Convention • IX. Pleasure

CHAPTER VI: Perfume 57
I. On Certain Perfumes • II. The Classification of Perfumes •
III. Perfume Criticism

CHAPTER VII: Time **65**
I. Time and Perfumes • II. The Time to Create • III. Time to
Sense • IV. Time to Buy • V. Time at Hermès

CHAPTER VIII: Marketing **75**
I. The Marketing of Demand • II. Niche Marketing •
III. The Marketing of Tomorrow • IV. To the Marketing People

CHAPTER IX: Bringing the Product to the Market **83**
I. The Manufacture of Perfume Concentrate • II. Perfume
Manufacture and Production • III. Safety Regulations •
IV. The Products • V. Concentrations

CHAPTER X: The Players on the World Market **93**
I. The Fragrance Industry • II. The Industry in Grasse •
III. The Perfumery and Cosmetics Industry • IV. Distribution

CHAPTER XI: Protection of Perfumes **101**
I. Protecting Names, Containers, and Packaging • II. Protection
of Fragrances

Perfumes and Their Creators. 107
Glossary 110
Suggested Reading 113

INTRODUCTION

If you had visited a perfume composer's laboratory in the early twentieth century, you would have found the perfumer—clad in a white coat—composing his products seated before a rack of primary ingredients, in a room saturated with fragrances. He had a close, physical relationship with his material. Formulas, like food recipes, were expressed in volumes: liters, deciliters, centiliters, and drops, sometimes a pinch. His utensils were phials, beakers, and droppers. His products: resinoids, absolutes, essential oils, dilutions, infusions—all derived from physical reactions with plants—and, even at that time, many chemical substances.

Today, my workplace is a villa. Nestled among white and gray rocks, it can seem like an austere spot. All that blooms there is a sprinkling of broom and lavender. The living room, with its wide windows, has been converted to an office and workshop. In summer, it is bathed in light, filtering through the branches of the parasol pines. In winter, it becomes melancholy, and the trees take on a golden green shade. From my office, in fine weather, I can see the Mediterranean Sea, bounded on the left by the alpine foothills of Grasse, to the right by the Esterel massif. When I am thinking and writing down the formula for a perfume, I work as far away as possible from the test laboratory, away from the products, to protect myself from their fragrances, which eventually impair your sense of smell. On my desk are dozens of tightly closed little bottles, paper, a few pencils, an eraser, and, in a vase, long, narrow strips of smelling paper—called blotters.

Using my olfactive memory, I select, write down, juxtapose, and dose dozens of aromatic compounds. Whether odors are good or bad doesn't matter; these materials are like words, I use them to tell a story. Perfume has its own syntax, its own grammar. My nose is nothing more than a measuring instrument. I use it to test, to compare, and to evaluate in order to mark, correct, and repeat the work in progress.

I am helped in my work by an assistant whose main job is to weigh the formulas to milligram accuracy, to monitor, manage, and check every material.

Chapter I

BIRTH OF MODERN PERFUMERY

Modern perfumery came into being at the end of the nineteenth century. Previously aristocratic and craft-based, perfumery was liberated by technological progress, the old methods supplanted by a victorious industry under the control of the bourgeoisie.

The perfumers of the time were Arys, Agnel, Bichara, Caron, Clamy, Coudray, Coty, Delettrez, Emilia, Felix Potin, Gabilla, Gravier, Grenouille, Guerlain, Gellé frères, Houbigant, Lenthéric, Lubin, Millot, Mury, Molinard, d'Orsay, Pinaud, Pivert, Rigaud, Rosine, Roger & Gallet, Violet, and Volnay. These names were often those of the business owners—chairman, financial director, production manager, and, of course, perfumer.

Whereas the standard products—dilutions, infusions, absolutes—continued to come from the factories of Grasse, these perfumers quickly grasped the benefits of chemical products, the molecules of scientific progress, that were made in France in the *usines du Rhône* and particularly in Germany by the firms Schimmel, Haarmann und Reimer. They had no hesitation in using them in their creations.

The perfumes were created, prepared, and packaged in factories around Paris. Most of the stores were on *rue Royale, rue du*

Faubourg Saint-Honoré, avenue de l'Opéra, and *place Vendôme,* or in the centers of big cities like Lyon, Lille, Bordeaux, and Marseille. They had outlets in the world's great capitals—Moscow, New York City, London, Rome, or Madrid.

At the root of this modern perfume industry was chemistry. By trial and error and by studying the components of essential oils, chemists created the first synthetic molecules. For example, in 1900, eight of the components of rose had been identified, twenty in the 1950s, fifty in the 1960s, and by the end of the twentieth century, more than four hundred. The standard synthetic products used today, such as aldehydes, ionones, phenylethyl alcohol, geraniol, citronellol, benzyl acetate, coumarin, and vanillin date from the first decade of the twentieth century, as do certain synthetic substances that do not exist in nature, such as hydroxycitronellal and the first musks.

For those early twentieth-century perfumers, synthetic products lacked the complexity of the natural products they were accustomed to. Although interesting, they were perceived as harsh, sometimes unpleasant. In response, the manufacturers of these substances created their own harmonious mixtures of natural and synthetic products, the early foundations of contemporary perfumery.

While the chemists sought primarily to understand nature, the perfumers experienced the use of synthetic products as a release from the compulsory reference to "nature," opening up new creative possibilities. Thus perfumer's amber, which is a dried-down component, has nothing to do with yellow amber, the fossilized resin, nor ambergris, the intestinal secretion of the sperm whale. It was the first fragrance to emerge from the invention of vanillin at the end of the nineteenth century. A simple combination of vanillin, a synthetic product, and labdanum absolute, a natural product, became an olfactory standard underlying a fantastic number of perfumes.

Sometimes favoring figurative, sometimes narrative creations, these early twentieth-century fragrances were simply named after flowers—*Rose, Pois de senteur, Violette, Héliotrope, Cyclamen*—or evocative names like *Ambre Antique* (antique amber), *Faisons un Rêve* (let us dream), *Quelques Fleurs* (a few flowers), *Cœur de Jeannette* (Jeanette's heart), *Chypre, N'aimez que Moi* (love only me), *Après l'Ondée* (after the rain), and so on. It was this creative uncertainty generated by scientific molecules— "artificial perfumes," as they were called at the time—that gave birth to twentieth-century archetypes.

In this artistic industry where France excelled, two men were particularly influential.

The first was François Coty. For this ambitious composer, perfume was primarily an object to be looked at. He met René Lalique, master glassmaker and jeweller who, like him, had a shop on place Vendôme. Their first collaboration was on *L'Effleurt* (1907), presented in the first bottle specially designed for a perfume. François Coty overturned tradition by showcasing a single perfume in his shop, innovated further with a catalog containing only twenty scents and summed up his beliefs in these few lines: "Give a woman the best product you can create, presented in a perfect bottle, of fine simplicity but impeccable taste, charge a reasonable price and you will witness the birth of a business such as the world has never seen."[1]

The second, Paul Poiret, was a famous fashion designer of aristocratic temperament. Aesthete, rebel, fantasist, demanding in his work, but a great party lover, he embodied the Dandy of the *"Belle Époque,"* full of *joie de vivre* and insouciance. Yet he understood the importance of branding his products. He would be the first fashion designer to establish licences on his products.

---

[1]E. Barillé, *Coty*, Paris, Éd. Assouline, 1995.

Under the *Les Parfums de Rosine* brand, he was the first fashion creator to engage a perfumer, a chemist by training, Maurice Shaller. Between 1910 and 1925, Maurice Shaller, and then Henri Almeiras, composed up to fifty original perfumes. The packaging came from Paul Poiret's School of Art—*l'Atelier de Martine*—named after one of his daughters. Most of the bottles were drawn by Paul Poiret himself.

This was the time when the links between fashion design, brand, and perfume were forged, never to be broken. In the early 1920s, the arrival of fashion designers such as the Callot Sisters, Gabrielle Chanel, Jeanne Lanvin, Jeanne Paquin, Jean Patou, Lucien Lelong, and Madeleine Vionnet threw the guild of perfumers into a ferment.

In the journal *L'Excelsior,* the fashionable writer Colette analyzed this alliance: "The fashion designer is better placed than anyone to know what women need, what will suit them . . . between their hands, perfume becomes a fashion accessory, an imponderable and indispensable flourish, the most essential of inessentials . . . perfume should represent the melodic theme, the clear, direct expression of the trends and tastes of our time."

In their fashion design business, the Callot Sisters offered their best customers several perfumes that were available exclusively in their stores. They answered to names like *Mariage D'amour, La Fille du Roi de Chine,* or *Bel Oiseau Bleu.* Gabrielle Chanel, whom Paul Poiret described as representing high-class miserabilism, approached the firm Rallet to supply a perfume she could offer her customers. Located at La Bocca near Cannes, this maker of raw materials for the perfume trade was the first to create fragrances on commission. In this firm she met her future perfumer, Ernest Beaux, and engaged Pierre Wertheimer, owner of Bourjois perfumes, to create her perfume. Chanel had already become famous for her taste for the plain, for simplicity. She expresses this belief in just a few words about her perfume and its container: "If I were a perfumer, I would put everything into the perfume, and nothing into the presentation . . . and to make it inimitable, I would want it to be extremely expensive."[2] *Chanel N° 5* was created in 1921.

Jeanne Lanvin acquired the services of the perfumer, André Fraysse, son of the perfumer from the French firm La Marquise de Luzy. He created *Arpège* in 1927 then *Scandale* in 1932. Another popular fashion designer, Jean Patou, engaged the perfumer Henri Almeiras, who had just left Les Parfums de Rosine and created for him perfumes that often bore American names like *Cocktail, Colony,* and *Joy.*

The most "productive" of the fashion designers/perfumers remains Lucien Lelong. His innovation was to showcase arrangements of perfume bottles, launching up to forty perfumes between 1925 and 1950. Finally, there was Madeleine Vionnet, the most innovative of the fashion designers, who created her designs directly on her clients. She branded her perfumes with the names of cities, repeated—*Paris, Paris; New York, New York; Milan, Milan.*

In 1925, at the International Exposition of Modern Industrial and Decorative Arts, perfumers and fashion designers sought to outdo each other in imagination. The dominant perfumers were Guerlain, who created *Shalimar* for the event; Lubin, who presented the eternal *Eau de Lubin;* Pivert, who offered the widest variety of products, *Les Parfums de Rosine,* from the great fashion designer Paul Poiret; and Coty.

In the 1930s, François Coty was king of the perfumers, but his extreme political beliefs and megalomania led him into debt. With his business tottering, he died at the end of the decade. The

[2]E. Charles Roux, *L'irrégulière*, Paris, B. Grasset, 1974.

Coty brand would survive in the United States, where it is today the best known of the mass-market fragrance brands. In Paris, under the influence of the American Elizabeth Arden and the Italian fashion designer Elsa Schiaparelli, bottles became figurative, sometimes bizarre, teasing or mocking. Out of friendship for Elsa Schiaparelli, the surrealist painter Salvador Dali designed *Roy Soleil:* the case is a golden shell that cleverly enfolds a bottle with a marine design. The stopper is shaped like the sun, with one of its rays dipping into the bottle for use as an applicator.

In 1931, the world economic crisis hit France. The arrival of the *Front Populaire* in 1936 revived old dreams. This was the time of the emergence of the first mass-market products: shampoos, suntan oils, and detergent powders, all imbued with odors that would remain in our memories.

In the aftermath of the Second World War, perfumes remained the province of the bourgeoisie. The big names were Coty's *Chypre;* Houbigant's *Quelques Fleurs;* Guerlain's *Mitsouko, L'Heure Bleue, Shalimar,* and *Vol de Nuit;* Caron's *Tabac Blond;* Chanel's *Nº 5;* Lanvin's *Arpège;* and Dana's *Tabu.* The new creations were *Femme,* launched through subscription by Marcel Rochas at the Liberation, a perfume created by the independent perfume composer Edmond Roudnistka; Piguet's *Bandit* created by Germaine Cellier; and *Miss Dior* by Jean Carles, both of them perfumers for the materials manufacturer Roure-Bertrand, which created perfumes for all the new fashion designers. Paris once again became the *mecca* of fashion. Perfumery followed *haute couture.*

In the 1950s, the dominant olfactory theme was lily of the valley, with Pierre Balmain's *Vent Vert,* Caron's *Muguet du Bonheur, Premier Muguet* by Bourjois, and Dior's enchanting *Diorissimo.* For men, strict, elegant fragrances were based on roots and wood with a *Vétiver* at Carven, Givenchy, and Guerlain.

Riding the wave of 1960s consumerism, the U.S. firm International Flavors and Fragrances (IFF) and the Swiss firms Firmenich and Givaudan engaged talented perfumers to develop their fragrance design centers, and created perfumery schools to train their future composers.

Research intensified, and the application of new analytical techniques, such as gas chromatography and mass spectrometry, made it quicker to identify components in flower extracts. These analytical tools were also used to study the competition and to decipher existing perfumes on the market. Designed by these methods, new, more synthetic perfumes, in turn, became the archetypes of future mass-market products.

In 1966, Christian Dior launched *Eau Sauvage,* garnering immediate international success. In its simplicity and rigor, this eau de toilette renewed the fragrance industry and gave rise to innumerable variants. Around the word "eau" there emerged a profusion of masculine, feminine, and androgynous aromas. Forty years after its creation, *Eau Sauvage* has lost none of its popularity.

The 1970s heralded the appearance of a new actor on the perfume stage: jewellers. Van Cleef & Arpels launched *First* in 1976 and Cartier brought out *Must* in 1981.

The luxury perfume market moved from an intuition-based approach—characterized by the choice of a dominant category of population on the basis of their lifestyle, the cult of the brand and the object, and restricted production—to "demand-based" marketing. This marketing approach analyzes the competition, the market, and the cultural, economic, and social environment. The strategy is to embody intoxications, fantasies, and passions through signs and symbols, and to create an object of desire. With the launch of Yves Saint Laurent's *Opium* in 1976, perfume broke the taboos of escapism and sensual delight. The perfume presents itself as mysterious and sacred, an embodiment of the eternal feminine. Inspired by Estée Lauder's *Youth-Dew* and launched with a big advertising budget, *Opium* was the French answer to the press campaign for Revlon's *Charlie,* launched three years earlier in the United States and the first perfume to seek to sell a lifestyle. In launching *Anaïs Anaïs* in 1978, the Cacharel brand expressed a different lifestyle, by commissioning the photographer Sarah Moon to evoke the duality of innocence and sensuality suggested by the perfume's name.

From this point on, the American model came to dominate the launch of many fragrances, with a focus on large advertising budgets offset by a 50 percent cut in expenditure on perfume concentrates. In order to meet the needs of the marketing gurus, manufacturers published the first perfume classifications and conducted market tests based on the analysis of customer profiles (see p. 80).

To meet production needs, extensive research went into the synthesis of natural products. New technologies, such as headspace analysis, were encouraged. Powerful substances such as the musks, originally developed for cleaning products, were increasingly used. Like "nouvelle cuisine," and as a consequence of greater use of synthetic products, the new perfumes improved in performance and stability. They also lost the thick, rich, and mellow character of earlier perfumes.

In the 1980s, "product" was everything: culture, literature, music, fashion, and, of course, perfumes. The dominant players were *Giorgio Beverly Hills* (1981), perfume of the stars, and Christian Dior's *Poison* (1985), with its theme of love and death. At the same time, after decades of use in detergents and fabric softeners, the odors of the molecules used in those products to convey a message of cleanliness became completely acceptable in fragrances. The prototypes of this simple, linear, recognizable, and identifiable olfactory message, largely aimed at men, was Guy Laroche's *Drakkar Noir* (1982) and Davidoff's *Cool Water* (1988) in Europe, and Calvin Klein's *Eternity* (1989) in the United States.

In the 1990s, ever responsive to trends, the marketeers adopted New Age, the spiritual movement born in California and Scotland, with its doctrine of mysticism as a source of personal well-being, a return to nature, and rejection of progress. With Estée Lauder's *New West* in 1988, then Calvin Klein's *Escape* (1991) and *Kenzo pour Homme* (1991), perfumers translated certain symbols of the spiritual movement—such as the sea and the ocean—into aromas. The market was overrun by a tide of marine scents.

In those years, because men and women felt lost in a world of confusion, there was an emphasis on identity in all spheres: religion, music, and clothes. It was expressed in layers of adornment, marks designed to signal one's membership of the same tribe. Calvin Klein took up and interpreted these signs in the advertisement for the unisex eau de toilette *ck One,* but by contrast with the 1960s, when unisex eau de toilette was experienced as an expression of community—for you *and* me—in 1994 the combination is perceived separately: for me *or* for you. With a pharmacy-style bottle, a message of nonpleasure to take the guilt out of the act of buying, and one's children "clean and equal," the focus had shifted to hygiene.

The consequence of political correctness was the emergence of a new conformity. Estée Lauder expresses the rebirth of tradition in the advertising strategy for his perfume *Beautiful* (1986) as does Elizabeth Arden with *True Love* (1994).

In response to these puritan values, France plunged into a sensual and greedy torrent of candy floss, chocolate, tea, figs, plums, praline, licorice, and so forth. The first perfume in this new trend was *Angel,* launched by Thierry Mugler in 1992.

Two cultures were locked in combat on planet perfume, the Latins versus the Anglo-Saxons.

Under the American influence, the research focus was the quest for *the* truth, and new techniques and tools—such as solid-phase microextraction (SPME) or CO_2 extraction—were developed to capture "nature."

Now, in the early years of the twenty-first century, France and the United States share the world's perfume market. Ten corporations hold 60 percent of the market. Certain perfumes dominate, forms have become similar, and the unique is rare. New products are launched all the time, product lifecycles have become shorter, packaging often more gimmicky, and advertising fundamental. Taste has become global, uniform.

Opposing or resisting this trend, new brands are emerging—firms like The Different Company, Diptyque, Éditions de Parfums Frédéric Malle, Serge Lutens, and L'Artisan Parfumeur. Without advertising or market testing, these "niche" perfumes are contributing to perfume's reinstatement as a luxury product and to the establishment of new objects of desire. In 2004, Hermès hired a perfume composer as its director of perfume design. In 2006, LVMH Group followed suit and in turn recruited a perfumer for all its brands. In 2008, Guerlain, after having discontinued the practice for a few years, reinstated a house perfumer. In these early years of the twenty-first century, many of the brands are placing a fragrance designer at the heart of their activity.

Chapter II

THE NOSE
AND ODOR

Nothing is more immoderate than an odor.
—JEAN GIONO

Of all the senses, the sense of smell is the most ubiquitous in the animal kingdom, whether in the air, in water, on land, or underground. Even bacteria have a sensory system for detecting odors. Although less powerful than in other animals (dogs, cats), the human sense of smell is closely involved in emotional life: intoxicating pleasure in the aroma of a wood fire, of a garment, of skin. The pain of the lingering fragrance left by those we have lost. The desire and pleasure aroused by a perfume, a wine, or a dish. Aversion to the sickly smell of hospitals. The warning smell of smoke, of gas, of pollution, and so on.

The sense of smell operates primarily at a distance, like vision, as a powerful system of detection, which contributes to individual and species survival. Here are a few facts that will give you a better understanding of this underrated faculty.

I. The Sense of Smell

The Olfactory Center. It is located in the upper part of each nasal cavity, which enables us to smell in stereo by means of the epithelium in each nostril, a tissue with a surface area of 2 to 5 cm² containing six to ten million olfactory nerve receptors. This is the first stage in our olfactory system.

II. The Olfactory System

1. Main Olfactory System. This system has three levels.

A. *The epithelium:* This area of tissue contains several million receptor cells. On each of these cells, dozens of cilia, loaded with receptor proteins, bathe in a thin layer of mucus. In order to be detected, odor molecules carried by the air we breathe must dissolve into this aqueous medium before settling (temporarily) on the cilia, which host chemical receptors. Each receptor cell expresses only one type of chemical receptor.

One remarkable property of these receptor cells is that they are regenerated every thirty to forty days, maintaining the permanence and quality of olfactory detection.

B. *The olfactory bulb:* The olfactory bulb is situated at the base of the cranium. It sits on a strip of bone, which is full of holes, through which pass the olfactory nerves linking it to the epithelium. As soon as the cilia capture a molecule, the chemical receptors are activated and send an electrical signal to the receptor cells that, via the olfactory nerves, converge onto specific regions of the olfactory bulb. The olfactory bulb then acts as a filter and partly identifies the information.

It condenses the information and sends it, via the olfactory tract, to the brain, where the information is processed.

C. *The brain:* The information is sent from the olfactory bulb, via the olfactory tract, to the olfactory cortex, which distributes it to several parts of the brain, such as the amygdala, the hippocampus, the thalamus, and the orbitofrontal cortex. Several of these structures belong to the limbic system, which is involved in processing memory and emotions. As smell is the only sense connected directly with the limbic system, odors have a strong emotional impact.

2. The Trigeminal System. As well as the main olfactory system, other sensory systems can also capture chemical molecules. One of these is the trigeminal system, which works in tandem with the taste and olfactory systems when we eat, and contributes to the sense of taste.

Completely separate from the olfactory bulb, the trigeminal system sends nerves into the nasal and mouth cavities and into the eye. It is stimulated by sharp, intense, burning, irritant tastes and smells, acting as an immediate warning system for chemical agents like acids, ammonia, and other toxic products. It is also this nerve that gives us the sense of spiciness, or the impression of coolness created by the smell and taste of mint.

III. Odor

1. Detecting Odor. While science is interested in the physiology of the sense of smell, the industry, faced with increasingly tough competition, seeks to master the techniques of perfume formulation in order to produce measurable and effective products. For this purpose, it has developed tools for measuring the previously unmeasurable—odor.

Since odor depends on the quantity of molecules present in the air and on the intensity of each one of them, companies have invented the notion of "olfactory value," a measurement based on the ratio between two other measurements: the vapor pressure and the detection threshold.

2. Vapor Pressure. This is used to measure the volatility of fragrant materials by quantifying the molecules emitted by means of headspace analysis. The vapor pressure is measured in ug/liter or microgram per liter of air (1 microgram=10^{-6} grams per liter of air).

For example, the vapor pressure of vanillin is low, at 2 ug/liter, making it a product with low volatility that lasts over time. By contrast, isoamyl acetate, which carries the aroma of banana, has a high vapor pressure of 24,000 ug/l and therefore fades in less than a minute.

3. Detection Threshold. This tells you the minimum concentration at which the odor is detectable. The method used to measure this is olfactometry. The detection threshold is measured in ng/liter or nanogram per liter of air (1 nanogram is the equivalent of 10^{-9} grams per liter of air).

For example, the detection threshold of vanillin is 0.02 ng/l, which means that vanillin is perceptible even in very diluted form. By contrast, the perception threshold of isoamyl acetate is low, at 95 ng per liter of air. Once diluted, isoamyl acetate becomes undetectable. However, it should be noted that the detection threshold varies greatly between people and that sensitivity to odors declines gradually with age.

Depending on the ratio between these two measurements, fragrant materials will be used for particular types of effect: diffusion, presence, or tenacity. These measurements have simply given perfumery an objective base, by measuring what perfumers already knew empirically through the practice of their craft.

4. Distinction. I know of nothing that has no smell. As an apprentice, I learned not only to distinguish between the odor of a jasmine concrete from Egypt, Italy, or Grasse in France, but to identify what kind of evaporator had been used to produce the absolute: one made of copper, tin, stainless steel, or glass. This final process of differentiation was so refined that it required comparative examination. With time, I learned the rounded fragrance obtained in copper, the elegant fragrance produced by tin, the metallic fragrance generated by stainless steel, and the bland fragrance created by glass. These examples show that, with a little training, a nose can easily tell the difference between odors.

We can all distinguish three or four flavors in a wine, and three or four fragrances in a perfume. For a professional, the threshold of differentiation increases tenfold. He can use this slowly acquired skill not just to create perfumes but also to make copies. While distinguishing between fragrances is not easy, identifying them is hard, as recognition is linked with memory. Of the ten thousand molecules developed by the perfume industry, a specialist can only really identify one tenth of that number.

5. Relativity. Since environments change, perceptions—whether visual, olfactory, aural, tactile, or gustatory—are always relative. Sensations are not independent of each other but linked with those that came before and those that accompany them, so that what we experience is connections between states. As there is no such thing as an "absolute nose," the result is that if we smell two different perfumes one after the other, we will not be able to judge them separately.

Connections between states are only useful when we are judging the performance, the quality of two versions of a single perfume.

6. Perception. Unlike detection, perception is the representation of an object constructed from sensation by consciousness. The perception of a fragrance varies from one individual to another depending on the degree of focus on the sense of smell and, obviously, on training and learning.

7. Increasing Sensitivity. Exercising our senses increases our sensitivity. Thus if someone is presented with a new taste for ten weeks, and the area of taste projections in the brain is measured regularly using MRI (Magnetic Resonance Imaging), we see an increase in the range of taste projections and an increase in sensitivity. In practice, we can all remember that twenty years ago, tea tasted so insipid that it was drunk as an infusion. Education and intense marketing around the drink have turned the French into a nation of tea connoisseurs. Specialist stores have opened, and there are enough teas now available to meet the varying demands of tea lovers, to the extent that French taste in tea has even crossed the Channel and earned respect in England. At present, a coffee machine brand is heading an educational campaign to familiarize us with the different tastes of coffee, with a view to establishing market dominance.

8. I Taste What I Know. When you see a tomato, red, round and shiny, you can almost taste it before you put it in your mouth. In fact, the brain can only see what it expects to see, can only feel what it expects to feel, and can only hear what it expects to hear. In fact, it even makes you hum a familiar tune slightly before you hear it. In the same way, many fragrances go unnoticed in the early stages after their launch. But by repetition, the message becomes obvious and, sometimes, ordinary.

9. Intensity. How do you define the intensity of an odor, of a fragrance? We talk of strong, powerful, intense fragrances or discreet, weak, light fragrances. The only physical method that has been found for measuring intensity is to dilute the smell or the perfume until it becomes imperceptible. This is because the power is inversely proportional to the concentration (see above—3. Detection Threshold).

Because a raw material or a perfume is at its maximum intensity in its pure state, the fragrance of a substance is assessed in dilution. Similarly, when developing a perfume, it is preferable to work in weak concentrations in order to detect the nuances. To identify a variation in intensity, the concentration of a raw material or perfume concentrate should be adjusted by a factor of at least 1:3.

10. Tenacity (long lastingness). How do you measure the tenacity of an odor, of a fragrance? The only known method is to test a blotter impregnated with the odor at regular intervals, minutes, hours, days, until you can no longer perceive the "shape" of the initial fragrance. The baseline measurement can be defined using a panel of "average" noses. This empirical measurement is obtained using a scale marked from 1 to 10. Each person specifies the level of perception. The average score for the group establishes the measurement.

11. Volatility. Other than measuring the vapor pressure using headspace analysis, another physical method is to weigh a blotter impregnated with a given weight of the relevant substance, at regular intervals, in order to establish an evaporation graph.

12. Recognizing a Perfume. When I notice a perfume in the street, I often confuse it with other perfumes. From a distance, I can identify its family from its trace in the air, but its odor is too imprecise to be identified with accuracy. The closer I get, the more clues there are, until I can finally name the perfume. In fact, while the perception of a model, based on its relevant traits, is enough to identify its family, only the content and the details enable me to distinguish it from other family members.

This ability to make a rapid judgement perhaps comes from our remote ancestors, for whom detecting a predator as quickly as possible was a matter of life and death. It may be that we developed ultrafast recognition procedures thousands of years ago based on the presence or absence of relevant characteristics.

For a composer of perfumes, the difficulty lies not in establishing a model, a sort of variation on a theme, but in creating prototypes that can become models.

Chapter III

MATERIALS
AND SUBSTANCES

*If you absolutely insist on the pure, unmixed song of the
nightingale, I recommend the synthetic nightingale.*

—JEAN GIONO

Since the words "material" and "substance" are easily confused, I prefer to start by defining how I will use them:

Material: any substance used to make or build.

Substance: a material considered from the perspective of its
properties and uses.

I. Materials of Natural Origin

When not produced in Europe, many materials are imported in
the form of essential oils, essences, absolutes, and concretes from
the four corners of the earth. They are extracted from the different parts of plants—flowers, buds, fruits, leaves, barks, woods,
resins, seeds, roots, and lichens.

These days, animal materials have been replaced by chemical reconstructions, with the exception of beeswax absolute, but
have retained the name of the "natural" odor, such as civet, castoreum (beaver), and musk (deer).

There are also "isolates," which are not strictly speaking products derived directly from a plant, but molecules that are characteristic of the odor of an essential oil, such as linalool, a constituent of the essential oil of rosewood; vetiverol, a constituent of the essential oil of vetiver; eugenol, a constituent of the essential oil of cloves, and so forth.

II. Techniques for Obtaining Materials

A great number of books have been written on the subject, so I will only provide a summary of the techniques most commonly used today.

1. Distillation. Many plants are capable of synthesizing and accumulating large quantities of essential oils in secretory cells. In the distillation process, the heat bursts these cells and they release fragrant substances that are borne along by water vapor. The mixture is condensed in a long, winding, rolled copper pipe, which is passed through a tank of cold water. As it leaves the coolant, the water loaded with essential oil is recovered in an *essencier* or decantation vessel. The water and essence separate automatically because of the difference in density. The product taken from the vessel is called essential oil. The decanted water is scented and can be used directly (rosewater, orange flower water, etc.).

The yield in essential oils can vary greatly depending on the plants being distilled. By way of example, 1 kg of essential oil requires 5 tons of magnolia blossoms, 4 tons of rose petals, 1 ton of bitter orange blossoms, 500 kg of clary sage, or 20 kg of lavender blossoms.

Historically, this most ancient of extraction processes was introduced into Spain by the Arabs in the ninth century, and came into use in France in the mid-thirteenth century. Since then, there have been many technical developments. These were achieved through close, often friendly, collaboration between perfume manufacturers and the boilermakers of the Grasse region, who have exported their technologies all around the world.

2. Extraction by Expression. This extraction technique is used exclusively for citrus fruits, because of the fragility of their essential oils. The expression process is largely carried out without heating, in situ in the citrus production regions (Brazil, California, Italy, Florida), by bursting the oil-bearing cells situated in the colored part of citrus peel.

In the eighteenth century, the essence was obtained by pressing the citrus peel manually and collecting it on sponges. Nowadays, the essence is extracted from the peel by mechanical scraping. Since the resulting product contains water, the essence is then separated from the water through decantation.

3. Extraction with Volatile Solvents. This process dates from the end of the nineteenth century. Shown for the first time at the Vienna International Exhibition in 1873, it made a great impression.

The process consists of leaving ground plants (such as wood, lichens, roots) or unprocessed plants (such as flowers, leaves, or resins), to macerate in a volatile solvent (hexane, petroleum ether, ethyl alcohol, etc.) in an extractor, then recovering the solvent with its perfume content. This solvent, with its processed plant fragrance, then goes into a concentrator where it is evaporated, recovered, and stored for further extractions. The residual product with its perfume content is called a concrete. This substance is stirred with ethyl alcohol in a beater then iced and filtered in order to separate the nonmiscible vegetable waxes from the perfume-bearing alcohol. An "absolute" is obtained after the final evaporation of alcohol. The yield is often higher than from distillation. Carried out at low temperature, this process avoids hydrolysis caused by water vapor and produces aromas that are closer to the initial odor of the plant.

Absolute yields vary depending on the plants processed. Thus, 1 kg of absolute requires 4 tons of tuberose flowers, 2 tons of violet leaves, 1 ton of rose petals, 800 kg de orange flowers, 600 kg of jasmine flowers, 300 kg of mimosa flowers, 100 kg of lavender blossoms, or 50 kg of oak moss.

4. Supercritical CO_2 Extraction. This extraction technique is of recent invention. When subjected to pressure of more than 73.8 bars and a temperature in excess of 88°F, carbon dioxide goes into a supercritical, liquid state. In this liquid state, it has good solvent properties. With CO_2 extraction, the raw material can be processed at a low temperature, producing an absolute that retains the original odor of the raw material. In addition, this process generates no pollution.

5. Costs. The selling price of a kilogram of essential magnolia flower oil is $935 at 2011 prices, as compared with $115 for essential oil of lavender, although more than 250 times as many magnolia flowers where required to produce it. This comparison shows that, with mechanical harvesting of lavender and a higher yield of essential oil, the price of an essential oil does not depend on labor costs, but essentially on demand.

III. Synthetic Materials

Based on petroleum and terpene chemistry, synthetic products are derived from benzene, toluene, naphthalene, phenol, and, in the case of terpenic compounds, turpentine. Most of these molecules are identical in structure to the natural molecules. They are often single compounds, which resemble natural odors, so they are easy to select and use. For example, phenylethyl alcohol, a major component of rose, resembles hyacinth, lily of the valley, and peony, all fragrances that—for technical and economic reasons—are not available as natural extracts.

The art of perfume is closely associated with chemistry. To illustrate the fact, I have listed the main synthetic raw materials used today in order of discovery.

1855
Benzyl acetate

1868
Coumarin

1874
Vanillin

1876
Phenylethyl alcohol

1888
The first synthetic musk

1889
Citronellol

1893
Ionone

1893
The methyl ionones

1903
The aldehydes

1908
Gamma-undecalactone
(peach lactone)

1908
Hydroxycitronellal

1919
Linalool

1933
Jasmone

1947
Irones

1951
Calone

1956
Lilial*

1965
Hedione*

1970
The damascones

1967
Galaxolide* (musk)

1975
Iso E*

*The names followed by an asterisk * are registered trademarks.*

By the end of the 1930s, all the major synthetic products used today had been discovered. Although most have been identified in nature, more than 30 percent do not exist in the natural state. Perfume chemistry can produce molecules that are not found in nature, but the fragrances chosen are usually variations on known odors, which foster a gradual evolution in taste.

IV. Analysis Techniques

In the mid-nineteenth century, analytic chemistry consisted in making the unknown substance react with known products in order to determine its nature. Today, we use methods drawn from physics in order to determine and quantify all the components, in a single operation.

1. Chromatography. Developed in the 1950s, gas phase chromatography (GC) is a technique that separates out molecules in mixtures that are highly complex in nature and have very varied levels of volatility. It is mainly used for gaseous compounds or compounds that can be vaporized through heating.

In the 1960s, this technique, in combination with mass spectrometry, made the identification of the components of essential oils much faster. For example, in essential oil of rose, fifty molecules had been identified in 1950, two hundred in 1970, and four hundred in the 1990s. Some of these molecules were then reproduced and became new synthetic products. Gas phase chromatography was also used to inspect deliveries of raw materials and, in the 1970s, to identify and quantify the known components in existing market fragrances.

Now miniaturized and relatively easy to use, GC is an analysis technique used in all perfumery laboratories.

2. Headspace. Headspace refers to a technique for analyzing odors. As its name suggests, this technique can be used to capture the most volatile odors. Headspace was originally a technique used to analyze the composition of gases in oil exploration. It was introduced into perfumery in the early 1970s.

In the technique, a gas is run across a plant—flower, fruit, leaf—in order to capture the odor-bearing components. The substances are caught in an absorbent filter and then analyzed and identified using a combination of chromatography and mass spectrometry so that they can be (re)constructed in the form of plant bases. These bases will be used in the composition of perfumes.

As well as offering a factual technique and approach to odors, this method claims to be able to objectively determine the aroma of flowers. Reason has taken possession of beauty, but beauty is not reason—it is emotion.

3. Solid-phase Microextraction. Even more portable and practical than headspace analysis, solid-phase microextraction or SPME employs a syringe fitted with a silica fiber impregnated with an ad hoc medium, which captures and concentrates the components of the odor under analysis.

This extraction technique requires neither solvents nor complicated equipment. The volatile components are absorbed, concentrated, and stored on the fiber, then analyzed by directly introducing the fiber into the injector of a chromatograph.

Invented in the early 1990s to monitor air and water quality, this highly portable technique quickly came to be used in identifying the fragrance of flowers and other odor-bearing sources. It has the further advantage of also being effective in an aqueous medium.

4. The Materials of the Future. Plants are chemical laboratories, producing an abundance of aromatic molecules. With genetic techniques, it may be possible to modify these natural laboratories to make biodegradable molecules identical to those in nature, for use in perfume production. By cutting the number of steps required to synthesize fragrances, this approach would protect the environment by reducing the amount of energy used in their manufacture. For the moment, this area of research is in its infancy.

5. Costs. The cost of synthetic materials is partly linked with the price of the original raw material, but primarily with the highly specialized and qualified—and therefore expensive—labor force (engineers, technicians) involved, and with the number of steps in the process of synthesis. Although the average cost of synthetic materials in 2011 is in the region of $42 per kilogram, costs vary, with iris-scented synthetic irone, for example, costing $4,675 per kilogram.

V. Substances

My collection grew from day-to-day work with the substance that we call odor, through attraction, through disappointment, through my own needs, and through the boundaries that I feel in each of them—in a word, through choice. Because to create is to choose. In the quest for a form of expression, for a style, the criteria used in selecting the materials of the collection were, to put it simply, the quality of the odor, its source, and its technical performances. Today, one-third of my collection consists of natural products and two-thirds of synthetic products. There are no base compounds in it.

The quality of the fragrance derives from a few simple criteria. It must have a single, clear character. For example, in the synthetic products, the only functions I have retained from the hexenol derivatives are alcohol and salicylate; from the phenylethyls, alcohol; from the benzyls, acetate and salicylate, although each of them has a dozen derived functions. For example, in addition to acetate and salicylate, the benzyl products contain propionate, isobutyrate, phenylacetate, butyrate, valerianate, and alcohol.

In products of natural origin, I exclude any product that lacks character. These include the essential oils of cascarilla, with its odor vacillating between nutmeg and clove, hyssop that oscillates between lavender and wild thyme, together with the absolutes of Karo-Karounde from Longoza, which is one of the characterless products used as filling. Although benzoin and Peru balms and resinoids are present, I use them rarely, since these odorants are foreign to my olfactory style. By contrast, the black currant bud absolute that appeared in the 1970s has a unique quality like no other in the palette of fragrances and immediately won me over. This product created the possibility for new combinations, new juxtapositions. Its use in Guerlain's *Chamade* (1969), then in Van Cleef & Arpels' *First* (1976), contributed greatly to changing taste in fragrances, as did the essential oil of magnolia leaves used for the first time in *Tocade* by Rochas (1994) or essential oil of pink pepper berries in Estée Lauder's *Pleasures* (1995).

1. Origin. The origin of a substance mainly matters with natural products. While the provenance alters the fragrance, I am more interested in the quality of the fragrance, which is primarily connected with the botanical variety of the plant. I chose Egyptian— or large-leaved green—basil, which contains 40 percent linalool, 30 percent methyl chavicol, and 10 percent eugenol, whereas basil from the Comoros Islands contains 80 percent methyl chavicol, which gives it an aniseed quality that does not interest me. Likewise, I selected lemon essence from Italy, which is livelier, essential oil of geranium from Reunion Island, which is peppery and rich, though sadly very rare.

2. Technical Performance. Cost, diffusion, tenacity, and stability are the other relevant properties of the substances in the collection. Of the twenty or so cedar fragrances on the market, four are enough for me. I use just one of the moss absolutes; among the methylionones, I find *Cetone Alpha*—a quality of methylionone known for its refinement—completely characterless and prefer a methylionone with a broader aroma at a fifth of the price. It is up to me to give it elegance.

Over twenty years, the criteria of quality, provenance, and technical performance have led me to reduce the number of fragrances in my collection from some one thousand raw materials to fewer than two hundred, a much more manageable quantity.

When I analyze the total number of components used in the ten creations I have launched in the last three years, I find that I have used no more than 130 in all. The fact that I have never used some of the raw materials in my collection does not mean that I have abandoned them. They are there, waiting, perhaps to be used, perhaps not.

3. The Collection and New Substances. Deciding which odors to choose when adding to the collection is difficult. Which product do you allow in from the dozen synthetic materials and the rare natural materials that become available each year?

Is the odor a new one? If not, can it replace an existing fragrance more cheaply, with comparable or even superior technical performance? Does it extend the olfactory range to which it belongs? These are a few of the questions I ask myself before admitting any new substance into my collection.

Products such as essential oil of magnolia flower, pink pepper berries, and absolutes of sambac jasmine and osmanthus have only come into perfumery in the last twenty years. Used in China as a fragrance in teas, drinks, or tobacco, they have now been adopted by the world of perfumery.

In any case, while the quality of a substance can contribute to the originality of a fragrance, a "fine" jasmine, a "fine" rose, or a "fine" synthetic molecule does not make a fine perfume. The beauty of a perfume does not arise from the sum of the qualities of the raw materials but from the harmony of the materials, the way they are used, juxtaposed, and given expression.

THE COLLECTION

Aldehyde C10	Artemisia e.o.
Aldehyde C11	Baies Rose e.o.
Aldehyde C12 L	Basil Egypt e.o.
Aldehyde C18	Beeswax absolute
Amarocite*	Benzoic aldehyde
Ambrettolide*	Benzoin resinoids
Ambroxide*	Benzyl acetate
Anethol	Benzyl salicylate
Angelica e.o.	Bergamot essence
Anisic aldehyde	Birch e.o.

Bitter orange e.o.
Black pepper e.o.
Black currant absolute
Bucchu leaves e.o.
Calamus Korea e.o.
Cardamom e.o.
Carrot seeds e.o.
Cashmeran*
Cassia absolute
Cassis base 345 B*
Cedar Atlas e.o.
Cedar Virginia e.o.
Celery leaves e.o.
Cétone V*
Cinnamic alcohol
Cinnamon Ceylan e.o.
Cis 3 hexenol
Cis 3 hexenyl acetate
Cis 3 hexenyl tiglate
Cis Jasmon
Cis-3 hexenyl salicylate
Cistus Spain e.o.
Citral
Citronnellol
Citronnellol L.
Citronnellyl acetate
Civet absolute
Clove e.o.
Coriander seeds e.o.
Corps jacinthe*

Coumarin
Cumin seeds e.o.
Cyclamen aldehyde
Damascenone
Damascone alpha
Damascone beta
Elemi e.o.
Ethyl acetyl acetate
Ethyl linalol
Ethyl maltol
Evernyl*
Florol*
Florydral*
Frambinone*
Fructone*
Gaïacwood e.o.
Gaiol acetate
Galaxolide 50% IPM*
Galbanum e.o.
Geraniol
Geranium e.o.
Globanone*
Hédione HC*
Hédione*
Hélional*
Heliotropin
Hydroxycitronnellal
Incense e.o.
Indole
Ionone beta

Iris concrete
Irisnitrile*
Iso E super*
Isobornylcyclohexanol
Jasmal*
Jasmin absolute
Jasmin Sambac abs.
Jasmolacton
Jasmonal H*
Juniper-berry e.o
L. rose oxyde
Labdanum resinoïd
Lavender e.o.
Lemon e.o.
Lilial*
Linalool
Linalyl acetate
Macrolide*
Magnolane*
Mandarin essence
Mate absolute
Melonal*
Methylcyclopentanolone
Methyl ionone gamma
Mimosa absolute
Musc t 93*
Muscénone*
Muscone*
Myrtle e.o.
Narcissus absolute

Néroli Artessence*
Nonenol cis 6
Nutmeg e.o.
Oak moss absolute
Octalactone gamma
Orange tree absolute
Orange e.o.
Osmanthus absolute
Paprika absolute
Patchouli e.o.
Peach aldehyde C14
Penny royal Mint e.o.
Petit grain
Phenylacetic aldehyde
Phenylethyl alcohol
Pimento berries e.o.
Rhodinol
Rhubofix*
Rose turkey e.o.
Sandalwood e.o.
Spearmint e.o.
Stémone*
Styrallyl acetate
Taget e.o.
Tarragon e.o.
Thyme e.o.
Tonalide*
Tonka bean absolute
Tuberose absolute
Undécavertol*

Vanilla absolute	Vetiver Haïti e.o.
Vanillin	Vetiverol
Veloutone*	Vetyveryl acetate
Verdox*	Violet-leaves absolute
Vertocitral*	Viridine*
Vertofix cœur*	Ylang-ylang extra e.o.

Names followed by an asterisk * are registered trademarks.
Names followed by e.o. are essential oils.

In order to prevent the collection deteriorating too fast, certain materials such as citruses and absolutes are kept refrigerated at a constant temperature of 50°F. The collection is renewed once a year. A first-use date is marked on each bottle as soon as it is renewed. I also find that warming compact materials such as resinoids, and absolutes in a water bath makes them easier to use.

VI. Formulation Methods

A fragrance formula is like a cooking recipe. The left-hand column lists all the materials, in no particular order. The right-hand columns specify the proportions of each ingredient.

Although there is software designed to help with the formulation process, I prefer to work on a sheet of paper with thirty lines and six columns so that I have a continuous overview of the formula, and also so that I can add comments of a technical or aesthetic nature, if necessary. I use the formulation software only to check prices and compliance (European legislation, IFRA, etc.—see p. 92).

1. Proportions. Although the priority is the juxtaposition of substances, the proportions of each component play an important role. To manage this, I use a base formulation quantity of 1,000 grams so that I can remember the proportions of each material used when creating a fundamental structure. I like to be generous with the products and quantities in order to give full expression to the formulation. Mean quantities generate mean ideas. My quantity scale is: 1, 2, 3, 5, 7, 10, 15, 20, 30, 50, 70, 100, 150, 200, 300, and so on. If I change the proportions of one or more materials, I always do so by a factor of at least 2.

Chapter IV

LEARNING
THE TRADE

*"Can you smell the chafer?", my grandmother used to
say when we were picking roses for the perfumeries. The
odor of the chafer was the sign of a good fragrance.*

When you enter a perfume laboratory for the first time, you
are assaulted by the smell. It is indescribable. It is just
there, overwhelming. It takes a while for the sense of sight to
return, and what you then see—lined up on glass shelves—are
hundreds of brown bottles of every size. They are stored in alphabetical order to make them easier to identify and use. This is
the collection you need to memorize to become a perfumer.

You do your learning in a separate room away from the
smells. You study the odors in sets of ten, each set at least one
hour apart. Each material is sampled on a blotter, in a 5 perent
dilution in 185°F proof ethyl alcohol.

Initially, odors of natural origin are easier to grasp—the substance smells of its name. Essence of orange smells of orange.
The names of synthetic products are less evocative. Benzyl acetate smells of benzyl acetate, reminiscent of English sweets or
banana. It takes a few months to realize that it is present in the
aroma of jasmine.

I. Odor Classifications

To help beginners memorize odors, different perfume companies have created various classifications. The one I provide is based around nine categories of odors.

1. Flowers. They are subdivided into five groups.
Rose flowers: This group, which includes rose e.o.[3], geranium e.o., and the odors of hyacinth, lily of the valley, and peony, is characterized by the fragrance of two components of these flowers—phenylethyl alcohol and geraniol.

White flowers: This group is determined by the combination of two molecules—methyl anthranilate and indole—that characterize the absolutes of orange flower, jasmine, and tuberose, but also the aromas of sweet pea, gardenia, and honeysuckle.

Yellow flowers: This group is defined by the presence of ionone beta, a molecule produced by the breakdown of the pigment carotene, which is responsible for the color of flowers like freesia and wallflower, extracts of which are in cassia absolute and osmanthus absolute.

Exotic or spiced flowers: This group is defined by the combination of benzyl salicylate and eugenol, which is present in the odor of carnations and lilies and as a component of in ylang-ylang e.o.

Anise flowers: This group includes mimosa absolute and the odors of lilac and wisteria. They are created using anisic aldehyde or heliotropin.

---

[3]e.o.: abbreviation for essential oil.

2. Fruits. They are subdivided into three groups.
Citrus: lemon e.o., bergamot e.o., orange e.o.
Orchard fruits: aldehyde C14 (called peach), fructone
(Soft) fruits: black currant absolute, frambinone

3. Woods. They are divided into five groups.
Sandal: sandalwood e.o.
Patchouli: patchouli e.o.
Vetiver: vetiver e.o., vetiveryl acetate
Cedar: Virginia cedarwood e.o., Atlas cedarwood e.o.
Lichen: oak moss absolute

4. Grasses. They are subdivided into three groups.
Green or fresh-cut grass: hexenol, galbanum e.o.
Aromatic: lavender e.o., rosemary e.o., thyme e.o.
Aniseed: basil e.o., tarragon e.o., anise e.o.

5. Spices. They are divided into two groups: cool spices and hot
   spices.
Cool spices: pepper e.o., cardamom e.o., nutmeg e.o., pink pepper
   rose e.o.
Hot spices: cinnamon e.o., clove e.o., pimento e.o.

6. Sweet Products. They are subdivided into three groups.
Vanillas: vanilla absolute, vanillin, benzoin resinoid
Coumarins: tonka bean absolute, coumarin
Musks: synthetic musks

7. Animal Products. They are subdivided into three groups.
Ambers: labdanum absolute, cistus e.o.
Castoreums: castoreum absolute, birch tree e.o.
Civets: civet, skatole, indole

8. Marine Products: seaweed absolute, calone

9. Minerals: aldehydes.

In addition to this classification, I recommend another system for identifying odors. To make it easier to memorize and to conceptualize "odor" as an object, I use words associated with another sense, in particular the sense of touch. So I say of an odor that it is hard, soft, cold, hot, velvety, dry, flat, sharp, silky, prickly, gentle, thin, heavy, light, harsh, fragile, oily, greasy, and so forth.

So the vocabulary specific to olfaction consists of words for aromatic objects (soap, sweet, cigar, etc.), of names of flowers (jasmine, lilac, lily of the valley, etc.), of names of chemical molecules (linalool, benzyl acetate, hexenol, etc.), or of their function (salicylate, aldehyde, etc.), and of words drawn from other senses.

However, what distinguishes the vocabulary of the perfumer from that of laypeople is the choice of a common language based on the training provided in perfumery schools and the discussions between perfumers and experts within the profession. This linguistic community creates a consensus around certain perceptual features. For the perfumer, soap, aldehyde, jasmine, nail varnish, rose, leather, wood, bonbon, and so forth are terms that describe the odor and not the object that produces it. A lily of the valley can be described as "jasmine," as can a fragrance, a washing powder, and so on. For the perfumer, the word "jasmine" refers to an olfactory experience, which can be very different from the fragrance given off by jasmine flowers. For the professional, therefore, the vocabulary of odors no longer brings to mind the image of the source but a mental picture of the odor. The perfumer thus invents the object of his science; he invents odor, and that is the source of his creativity.

This is reminiscent of the emergence of the language of color from so-called "primitive" cultures through to industrial civilizations. Certain cultures in Africa have not developed a specific language to name colors and simply organize their world around dark and light. In these cultures, the description of color sensations draws on vocabulary from other senses (colors are dry, wet, soft, hard, dull, etc.) or simply on the colored object (objects are the color of certain leaves or of the sky at sunset before the rain, etc.). By contrast, in our industrialized culture, the use of color to discriminate between objects is expanding, becoming not the only but the most accessible of the characteristics used to distinguish objects (New York's yellow cabs, the Hermès orange box, etc.).

II. Memorizing the Collection

When we think about these examples drawn from the language of color, it is obvious that there is no need for the object—the thing—to be given a name, for it to exist in the memory. The same is true for odors. However, it is useful to draw up a list—an inventory of the olfactory memory—in order to identify its failings, its deficiencies. To do this, I use a big table and a few sets of spare business cards. I write the names of the materials in the collection on the back of these cards, one card for each name.

In the first exercise, I group the names of the substances by their olfactory similarities, without smelling them, working solely from my memory of each material's fragrance. I order them on the table into "olfactory fields." These olfactory fields are not categories of odors that I can group under a single word, as I could with olfactory categories, but are sets of odors that have linked fragrances. There is no limit to the number of olfactory fields.

In the second exercise, I assemble the odors by their olfactory similarity, after having smelled each of the materials in the collection in dilution in small bottles. I smell the whole collection blind, without reading the name of the product, because only the odor matters, then I construct new olfactory fields. When I do this, I become aware that I have difficulty in ordering some of the names of the materials that I use, that their olfactory outline is vague in my memory. I carry out this olfactive inventory in successive stages, working one hour per day.

III. Type of Olfactory Field

1. Referential Communication. In my search for a vocabulary of odors, I worked with the Catholic University of Louvain-la-Neuve in Belgium, which specializes in cognitive science and the structure of knowledge, and developed a learning game that makes the language of odors more accessible.

Setting up the game. Two people sit opposite each other, each with an identical set of five to seven small bottles containing a 5 percent dilution of raw material in ethyl alcohol. One collection is labeled in alphabetical order (A, B, C, D, E, etc.), the other numbered (1, 2, 3, 4, 5, etc.). The "umpire" is the only person who knows the name of the materials and takes care to ensure that the odor in bottle A is not the same as that in bottle 1, since the bottles must be labeled in random order. To play the game, the two participants familiarize themselves with their collection and establish correspondences. For example: A=3, B=1, and so forth, exclusively by verbal description. At the end of the exercise, the names of the materials are revealed.

This game can be used to memorize fragrances, but also as a tool for learning the vocabulary of odors.

2. Models. I recommend that learners create odor notebooks with two entries: the name of the material and the name of the odor it brings to mind. For example, angelica e.o. corresponds to iris roots, gentian corresponds to angelica e.o., and iris corresponds to angelica e.o. I also recommend notebooks for recording performance (intensity, long-lastingness, volatility, stability) and sensory qualities (odors that are bright, dark, dense, thin, light, heavy, soft, harsh, warm, gentle, etc.).

The learning process continues with the copying of perfumery models, as in all artistic disciplines. Initially, the models are the bases that form the milestones in perfumery history, then perfumes that are particularly characteristic of their era. All this imitation drives home the importance of the interactions between materials, the role of the fragrance's total construction, and the choice of substances, not forgetting the role of the meaningful detail. As the philosopher François Dagognet puts it, objects are repositories of what we can learn about people. Like all objects, perfumes contain a wealth of information: the taste and the aesthetic norms of the era when they were created, the relationship with the body that is expressed through their use, and the safety rules and technical knowledge entailed in their production.

3. Perfumery Schools. Perfumery schools first emerged in the 1960s, in response to growing consumer demand for fragrant products. They were initially created by firms in the industry, the best known being Roure in the south of France and Givaudan in Switzerland. The year 1970 saw the creation of ISIPCA—the *Institut supérieur international du parfum, de la cosmétique et de l'aromatique alimentaire*—in Versailles. Since then, other schools have established courses in perfumery techniques, mostly in the context of day-release contracts with perfume companies. Out of the hundreds of candidates who apply every year, each school selects no more than twenty students. And out of all the schools, less than a dozen students will become perfumers. The others will find jobs as cosmeticians, evaluators, marketing assistants, quality controllers, production managers, and the like.

Chapter V

THE TRADE

Speak not of what you feel but of what you remember.
—J. JOUBERT

I. From Know-how to Science

As a lab assistant to perfume designers, I was exposed to different—often complex—ways of formulating fragrances (this stage is no longer part of the perfumer's training). As an apprentice, I learned things that would help me to fulfil the demands of international markets, aided in particular by the use of the then recent technology of chromatography. I was fed on a steady diet of market analyses and odor analyses: essential oils, bases, and perfumes. In my formulations, I combined materials and believed, naively, in the molecule that would change everything and would finally prove my creative talent. In my search for a style—since I still knew nothing about constructing a perfume—I tended to avoid complex formulations. The turning point came when I read a little illustrated booklet with a bouquet of flowers on a black background on the cover. The firm Dragoco had dedicated the whole of their journal *Dragoco Report* to the perfumer Edmond Roudnitska. The subject was: *The young perfume composer and odors.* Although dated 1962, the approach was new. He spoke of beauty, taste, simplicity, method, in smelling and judging, but also of erudition and of his philosophy of life. He became a part of my life, to the point that I have long held a secret desire to be called, like the subject of the book, a "composer of perfumes," although on his business card he contented himself with the title "perfumer." I imitated the perfumes created by Edmond Roudnitska. Chromatographic analysis gave me most of the components, but there were many ways of interpreting them. I was attracted to his writings and to the fragrance of his creations, which became objects of knowledge. I needed to strip them bare to experience them properly and make them my own. I saw them as blueprints, a rigorous design process, one fragrance corresponding to one effect. Stripped of affectation, of superfluity, the construction was expressed openly and the perfume could breathe. This approach led me to rethink my own methods of formulation. Formulation ceased to be a question of combining odors, but of shaping, in other words building and composing, by creating relations between odors. To illustrate this approach, I often quote the German philosopher Leibniz: "Because the sound of the sea is a whole, in order to hear the sound, we have to hear the parts that make up that whole, in other words, necessarily, the sound of each wave, even though each of those little sounds can only be heard in the confused whole of all the other sounds."

Edmond Roudnitska's creative approach could be summed up in Paul Cézanne's phrase "to have sensations and to read nature." So when headspace technology arrived in the late 1970s, I became an immediate convert. With this process, you can extract the odor of flowers, of rare plants, *in situ*, analyze them, and then reconstruct them. It was like having a snapshot of the odor, which would allow me to surpass the master.

This technology revealed the complexity of the odor of plants. Nature is full of surprises! Four hundred molecules for a jasmine, five hundred for a rose. It also showed that while the composition of a flower's odor varies according to the time of day, the flower's generic character remains unaltered.

This latter observation led me to think that the character, the shape of an odor, arises from its component materials, rather than the proportions used. From here, it was a short step to making the link between the odor of a flower and the shape of a perfume, and I changed my method of formulation.

Since then, I have focused on the choice of materials, often changing proportions considerably. I am careful to avoid overlaps.

I use fewer materials in my collection.

When I created Van Cleef & Arpels' *First* in 1976 at the age of twenty-eight, my nose was nourished on existing models. The source of the creation was internal, in knowledge and intellect. And although based on a smaller collection, the shape of this perfume was complex. With Sisley's *Eau de Campagne* in 1974, and a few other perfumes for L'Artisan Parfumeur, although the tomato flower theme arose partly from digression and intuition, it was not until the early 1990s that I moved deliberately into the unknown. Models belong to their era and, like fashion, become outmoded. In order to avoid this, I had to remain an apprentice, remain curious about the world, and continue to seek in the hope of finding.

Since then, every year, I have started a new Moleskin notebook where I record pretexts, ideas, simple connections, thoughts, quotations, and sketches of formulas. What goes into it is the people I meet, my journeys in the outer and inner world, the times in which we live, and not the analysis of market trends.

II. Finding a Pretext

I am a pilferer, a thief, a scavenger of odors. For me, nature is a pretext—a starting point, and not a source, of inspiration or creative insight. Sunsets or sunrises are beautiful wherever they are. It's only a question of perspective, of point of view. In a perfume, I do not create surprise by faithfully reproducing the aroma of tea, of flour, of figs, as they are. To create is to interpret odors by changing them into signs and for these signs to convey meaning. The odor of green tea becomes a sign for Japan, flour signals skin, mango signifies Egypt. More than the know-how, it is the style, the taste of the creation, that is personal to me, and although imitable, this style cannot be taught. In that respect, it becomes an art.

For *Eau Parfumée au Thé Vert* from Bulgari, created in 1992, I chose the tea theme well before I visited the *Mariages Frères* stores, on *rue du Bourg-Tibourg* in Paris. It was only later that I went there, in order to smell all the teas, to confirm my concept, and to be able to speak of a reality I had experienced, to give this creation plausibility. With *Bois Farine* from L'Artisan Parfumeur, created in 2003, it was the flour-odor of the flowers of the Ruiza Cordata tree on Reunion Island that made the perfume feasible. The theme, however, came from a note that I had captured when smelling a packet of "Francine" flour. The idea of wood came from my love of Reunion Island where the inhabitants give places the names of woods: green wood, stinking wood, yellow wood, and so forth. However, the shape of the perfume remained to be found.

With *Un Jardin sur le Nil* for Hermès in 2005, I chose the theme during a walk on one of the garden islands on the Nile at Aswan. The idea came to me in an alley of mango trees. It was May. The branches of the mango trees drooped under the weight of green fruit, which was within my reach. I picked one. A transparent milk flowed from the receptacle. I held it to my nose. The odor seduced me. A profusion of fragrant images, of resins, of orange peel, of grapefruit, of carrot, of opoponax, of juniper, an odor that was sweet and sour, vivid and mild. I gave in to it, let the odor caress my senses and take possession of me. I tried to share my pleasure, my feelings, with the people around me. I had my theme.

Long before this walk I had rejected the scents of jasmine, of orange flower, of spices, of all odors that imprison Egypt in the stereotyped mythical aromas of the Orient as seen through Western eyes.

What I was looking for was an original way in to the story of that garden. The odor of the green mangoes became a symbol of the garden islands of the Nile. Later on, I learned that in Egypt there is an annual festival celebrating this fruit.

While choosing a pretext is crucial, what I am trying to explain here is that I cannot create without having a catalog of illusions of odors in my head, a catalog that I can modify and order to my needs.

III. Olfactory Illusions

I am not interested in reproducing nature in its complexity. What I love is the process of internalizing and transforming it to my taste, conveying it in a few traits by the arrangement of a handful of fragrant materials. This is the alpha and the omega of the understanding of relations between odors, the basis of all olfactory illusions. Illusion is more true than reality. The plausible is more believable than the true. I need to describe the reality of these processes, although few people have the materials required to participate. What I am explaining here is a semantics of smell. Odors are not like words or musical notes, which follow each other in Indian file to form a sentence or a melody and thereby create meaning. The materials of fragrances do not mix like colors to create a new color. Instead, they coexist and continue to express themselves individually while at the same time forming a new odor, a new meaning. In olfactory terms, $1+1=3$, and 1 remains perceptible. To create these olfactory illusions, you play a kind of game in which you hold a minimum of two blotters impregnated with diluted materials (see below, odor of apple) to your nose and shake them like a slightly open fan. Sometimes, to reduce the intensity of a material, one blotter is held slightly further away. These illusions are not models, just olfactory illustrations of the movement of thought, which seeks only to invent and to be renewed.

	Apple	Peach	Pear	Strawberry	Wild Strawberry	Raspberry
Fructone	+	+	+	+	+	+
Aldehyde C14		+				
Black currant absolute		+				
Benzyl acetate	+					
Geraniol			+			+
Hexyl acetate			+			
Ethyl maltol				+	+	+
Methyl anth.					+	
Ionone beta						+

Diagram of olfactory illusions: Dip each blotter lightly in the products and shake it under your nose.

Illusion is not a lie, it is a way of fulfilling desires.

IV. Writing Down a Perfume

How many times have I found or invented reasons to put off the moment of putting down the first words on the blank page, the names of the materials, which are supposed to express the idea that began with a pretext! Tidying the little bottles of work in progress that are scattered across my worktable; a glance at an unanswered letter; an unidentified noise; waiting for a telephone call.

This "composer's block" can last for hours, for days. In fact, what I want is for the first draft to be perfect, to contain everything I want to express, already to possess the texture of its final form, so that I can fine-tune the idea, the theme, for several days, several weeks, although I know from experience that it is better to put down on the page something, however imperfect, that at least has the merit of existing.

However, composing a perfume is different from other forms of expression, such as writing or music, where words or notes are put down in a continuous sequence. You do not find this successive and ordered arrangement of words or musical notes in the composition of a perfume because the components that go into a perfume formula, whether fleeting or long-lasting, are perceptible at once in their entirety. The olfactory impression is total since the materials of perfume fade over time. Hence the error, too commonly taught, of dividing up a perfume into head, heart, and base, which is essentially an analytical approach—a deconstruction. Essential oil of bergamot, which is considered to be a head note, lasts for six hours on the blotter; phenylethyl alcohol, a so-called heart note, twenty hours, and musks for several days; whereas the fragrance of an eau de toilette should last no more than six hours. That is why I advise against this type of construction, even if the order of evaporation on the blotter and on the skin suggests a kind of linearity in the components.

I am often surprised by what I create and, while the idea may be present from the first attempt, the form I had imagined and that drove me on is often disappointing. The way I compose my formula, the choice of substances, the unexpected shape I drift towards until I reestablish control, are obviously linked with knowledge, with a form of intelligence and sensibility, but also with intuition—which I see as unconscious knowledge—and with an attitude. An attitude that I define as that of a curious, creative mind, a mind that cultivates perseverance, doubt rather than certainty, rejecting convention, and seeking pleasure above all.

V. A Curious Mind

While experience has taught me that certain materials are naturally singular, sometimes difficult to use, there are no bad or good odors, just substances I work with. A substance without beauty, without apparent quality, except something that I half sense could contribute to the beauty of a perfume. And although small, my collection of materials is large enough to develop and maintain a sense of curiosity, a permanent quest for possibilities, for the new in the old and for the unexpected in the familiar.

VI. A Creative Mind

When I write down a perfume formula, not only do I have a global vision of what I want to achieve, but I memorize the substances and the likely role of each one of them in the composition. Pascal's reasoning—"I cannot understand the whole if I do not know the parts and I cannot understand the parts if I do not know the whole"—is an idea that encourages me to shuttle constantly back and forth in my thinking.

In addition, because I have a taste for virtuosity, which is a form of seduction, I always seek to minimize the use of resources. However, all this is simply expertise, skill, and the aptitude required to set the mind free, to be creative.

Creativity is partly a matter of associations of ideas. When I rub geranium leaves between my fingers, of course I smell geranium, but also black truffle, which in turn evokes the taste of olive oil, and this reminds me of the odor of castoreum, which has the smoky aromas of birchwood. The association between birchwood and geranium sets up interesting connections. The most remote associations are often the most interesting ones.

Below is an odor map, which is like a heuristic representation of different olfactory links with possible connections.

It may seem paradoxical, but creativity is linked to forgetting. We all have books that we enjoy reading and rereading, which are always the same, but each time they seem slightly different; paintings that we know intimately, yet in which we discover a detail that alters our perception; a photo that betrays our beliefs about the past. It is this ability to forget that is one of the things that distinguishes us from computers and enables us to evolve, to see differently. It is because I can forget that I was able to shift the characteristic odor of ionone beta—a synthetic substance whose name and odor had for a century been associated with violet—into Bulgari's *Eau Parfumée au Thé Vert*. Combining ionone with hedione, another synthetic substance, evokes the aroma of tea. The components of a perfume are like the words of a language. They evolve over time—with their time—and can take on new meanings.

VII. Perseverance, Certainty, Doubt

It takes perseverance to put together a formula, given an eau de toilette that contains twenty to thirty ingredients can contain proportions as small as just a few PPM (parts per million) and as large as a few hundred grams and given that each component interacts with its own intensities, volatility, and lastingness. You have to be ready to try and fail over and over again.

Perseverance is essential in view of the fact that, in normal working conditions, the waiting time between two olfactory judgements varies from fifteen minutes, in the case of an addition to a work in progress, to more than an hour when assessing the whole formula, diluted in alcohol at the desired concentration, checked through a blotter test, then rechecked for several hours at regular intervals. In all, the journey from the first draft to the completed composition can take anywhere from a few months to a year of day-to-day effort.

In order to overcome the initial inertia, the gut refusal to compose, which is a form of flight—in order to act—it is useful to cultivate a short-term sense of certainty because creating a perfume is above all a matter of commitment, built up and patiently maintained day after day. Certainty, too, in order to set free your intuition and to be bold in the choice of ideas, in the arrangement of components and their proportions.

At the same time, you need doubt to avoid becoming complacent. Doubt gives you the necessary distance not to judge test compositions too hastily. It protects you from immediate satisfaction, the intense moment of pleasure, which may be overturned a day later when you sample the fragrance again. Doubt is of equal importance in synthetic and analytic perception.

VIII. Rejecting Convention

Despite my fondness for familiar perfumes, and for the flagships of international good taste, I feel that a certain distance from the markets can protect you from emotional compromise. Out of a combination of curiosity and critical withholding, I respond to all this olfactory noise by personally seeking out unexpected odors. For example, a perfume's theme can emerge not only from the rediscovery of a substance but from the attraction to a potential signal such as the odor of a fabric, of tar, of a wood, and so forth. From the emotion aroused by the scent of a gardenia in the rain or perhaps from the reworking of a fragrance that I like.

IX. Pleasure

Pleasure is selfish. Luxury is something you share. The aim of perfumery, as of all the arts, is to create products that arouse sensual pleasure. As a man and as a composer of perfumes, I must feel pleasure in order to give it. The pleasure of surprising, of evoking, of suggesting, of hinting. Perfume is a story in odors, sometimes a poetry of memory.

With *Un Jardin en Méditerranée,* created for Hermès in 2003, my pretext came to me in Leila Menchari's garden in Tunisia, on the shores of the Mediterranean. The story began simply—the sight of a smiling young woman tearing up and sniffing a fig leaf. In capturing that moment, I made a choice, the odor of the fig leaf became a symbol of the Mediterranean.

A few days later, back in my laboratory, I composed the main outlines of this perfume, emerging from the experience of a shared emotion, and using my notes to jog my memory.

Of course, I could have used the sophisticated *headspace* technique to sample the ambient odor of the garden. However, this way of doing things is like taking a snapshot, a soulless photograph that reveals nothing about the emotional tone of a place. That instrument is only a red herring, a simulacrum of nature, an obsolete artifice that represents nothing more than a pale imitation of perception and lived emotion. Using this analytical method to try to recreate figurative perfumes, real odors reminds me of those nineteenth-century perfume recipes, with their scent of rose, of clover, of violet—pretty mixtures, but not compositions, creations of the mind.

Headspace, an analytical method of which I was a great fan, has shown its limitations in the quest for new materials: after twenty years of analytical research, it has given perfumers fewer than a dozen molecules. These days, it is primarily used in sales materials. The substances of the future will come mainly from pure research and human imagination, not from the mechanical capture of nature.

Stemone and gamma-octalactone are two components that can suggest the odor of fig leaves. But the shape of the perfume cannot be reduced to the combination of the two materials that create the note. In perfume, construction and composition are closely linked. Construction can be defined as the balance between the intensities and masses found in the basic note. Composition, for its part, is expressed in the play of connections, of contrasts, of variance, and of overlaps. Thus stemone, with its aroma of crumpled mint leaves, combined with the fruity plum fragrance of gamma octalactone, together suggest fig leaf, while adding iso E gives a woody, nervy, spicy structure, and hedione a fresh, flowery lightness. Stemone and gamma octalactone are very intense materials whereas iso E and hedione create their effect through their proportions. This combination of intensity and proportion balances out to create the aroma of fig.

It is the composition that expresses the interplay generated by all the combinations of substances, and it is by seeking a pattern, a melody, that I create an olfactory form. When form takes on meaning, then I experience the excitement of the moment, the pleasure of composition guided solely by intuition. Sometimes, the form remains hidden and escapes me. In this case, a few days spent working on other projects helps me to find my way again.

After numerous attempts, multiple combinations of chords, and through the interplay, accumulation, and selection of associated ideas, the form becomes a perfume. And that perfume becomes the poetry of the memory of a Mediterranean garden. To make it surprising, clear, and bright, I favor black currant and bergamot notes over the dried fruit character of the fig, which would give the fragrance a heavy, rich, foodlike quality. I choose a vegetal accord, a harmony of wet, crumpled vegetation, and a spark of sharp freshness and bitterness in the orange note. Finally, I consider the volume, the diffusion, and the aura of the perfume, an impression more important than persistence.

You have to feel pleasure in order to arouse and move others. The special pleasure of perfume, which can be renewed constantly through a single gesture.

Obviously, this is a process that can continue indefinitely. I can always add details and lose my way. I avoid this risk when I think that I have answered all the questions that were in my mind in creating the perfume, but also when the subjective approval of a very small committee is achieved.

Thus the composition of a perfume is not only the outcome—sought, chosen, and unique—of the "conflicts" and "fusions" between the different substances involved in the process of construction and composition, as I have tried to show, but also the expression of an olfactory style, an artistry, the art that I have of thinking "outside the box," which is the mark of every composer of perfumes.

Chapter VI

PERFUME

In Art, everything is a sign.

—P. PICASSO

Every day that I work with perfumes I am in search of beauty, yet I still don't know where it is to be found. What I know is that in order to enchant you, to charm you, to tempt you, to influence you, to fascinate you, in a word, to win you over, I have to manipulate and make a show of what I know, to make the perfume desirable. Desirable—the adjective that for the classical philosophers marks the limitation of art. However, the fact that perfume evaporates and disappears is proof that it cannot be possessed—desire remains desire.

So it is through the use of memory, through the remembrance of shared fragrances, that I create the seductiveness of perfumes.

Deliberately or spontaneously, beginning in the womb and throughout our lives, we fashion our olfactory memory by repeated acts. As we grow, olfactory memories become part of our emotional life. That is why we like the smell of our children's skin, our partner, clean towels, a scarf, an old cardigan, nail varnish, buttered toast, jam, coffee, tea, chocolate, vintage wine, almonds, nutmeg, pepper, thyme, rice, Petit Brun, flowers, fruit, honey, lavender, pencils, glue paste, waxed furniture, cut grass, and rain. And why, by contrast, we dislike the smell of unwashed sheets, sour milk, cooked cabbage, garlic, certain paints, stale tobacco, the subway, bleach, blackboard rubbers, cat pee, and wet dog, especially someone else's dog. And although the difference between a pleasant or unpleasant smell is sometimes simply a matter of personal history, associations with meetings, with happy or painful events, we have common memories that enable us to share emotions.

Since olfactory memory determines our choice of perfumes, for the composer of perfumes our olfactory recollections become objects of desire. Contrary to popular belief, therefore, the sense of smell is not vague and rudimentary, but a complex and accurate faculty, to the point that the brain is able to use a few fragments of olfactory information, conveyed by a handful of molecules, to reconstruct the total image of an odor, provided—of course—that it is remembered. Which is remarkable but also an illusion. The pleasure of the senses is also an intellectual choice.

I. On Certain Perfumes[4]

In order to judge perfumes that have outlasted time I use today's nose, whereas for new perfumes I use yesterday's nose. And I realize that memory works in such a way that perfumes, which are not experienced with excitement and passion, which are not linked with a personal story or, in our business, with the training of the nose, are devoid of meaning and leave no trace in the memory. I thus conclude that evaluation by categories, by classification, is not enough for me. This perception of perfume is too analytical, too distanced, to move me. In order to discover a perfume, I have to enter into it and grasp it from the inside. Once

---

[4]This title is taken from the last piece written by Jean Giono.

it is separated from its external apparel, I can appraise, judge, and decide.

I also notice that my perception, my understanding, and my judgements of perfumes have evolved with the ideas, the values, the customs, and the tastes of society, and that the mental picture I have of perfumes has constantly altered and become richer. This means that I am constantly reinventing my representation of the past—the past that builds my future creations.

Osmothèque[5] enchants me with L. T. Pivert's *Trèfle Incarnat* (1905), which smells of progress in its massive use of amyl salicylate, its steely odor, and with Guerlain's *Après l'ondée* (1905) and its audacious use of anisic aldehyde, evoking mimosa and frangipani.

It is a great surprise to discover the perfumes of Paul Poiret (1910–1925), his early use and abuse of aldehydes, from the most metallic to the most fruity, from the abstract odors in *Arquelinade* to the figurative fragrances of *Fruit Défendu*; and while these forms sometimes lacked balance, harmonies, they all have *chutzpah*, which delights me.

Pleasure is the keynote of the perfumes of my generation created between the 1950s and 1970s. They have names like *Bandit, Fracas, L'Air du temps, Diorissimo, Eau sauvage, Fidji, Calèche, Habit Rouge, Calandre, Chamade, Nº 19*. They have a smoothness, a thickness, a roundness, a complexity, a richness, a softness, and a collection of values that I call "greasiness," which comes from the deliberate use of natural products, which envelope them, create a "material" effect, and give them their signature.

The pleasure becomes sensual, almost carnal, when I smell Guerlain's *Shalimar*, Estée Lauder's *Aromatics Elixir* or *Youth-Dew, Miss Dior, Eau d'Hermès*, and Yves Saint Laurent's *Opium*.

---

[5]Osmothèque: perfume conservatory; 36, rue Parc de Clagny, 78000 Versailles.

As regards the novelties of the twenty-first century, they can sometimes delight through their audacity and their capacity to surprise the nose.

So each generation builds its roots and its sense of identity, whether in clothes, music, scents, and so forth. Perfume is a product of society and, in this sense, is condemned to die if its myth and its memory are not maintained, not in the past but in a message that is constantly renewed, recomposed, sometimes—most often—through advertising, through a discourse that emphasizes neglected aspects, but also by the renewal of existing themes. Rose is undoubtedly the subject to which composers of perfumes returned most often in the twentieth century.

II. The Classification of Perfumes

While the idea of defining odors goes back to Aristotle, that of grouping and classifying perfumes emerged in the late twentieth century, as the fragrance industries sought to delineate the complex world of perfumes, to establish an inventory, and in some cases to look for the nonexistent. In 1976, the German firm Haarmann & Reimer proposed the first classification of women's perfumes, based on genealogies, families of perfumes inspired by the model classification produced by the firm Grayson Associates Inc. in the United States. Since then, others among the big market players have followed suit with their own classifications.

The best known and the benchmark for the whole perfume industry is the classification established by the *Société Française des Parfumeurs* and published in 1984. Initially, it was restricted to women's perfumes and divided into five big olfactory families: floral, chypre, fougère, amber, and leather, which apart from the fougères and the leathers, were further divided into several subfamilies. The second classification was published in 1990. As well as the classification of women's perfumes, it includes one of men's fragrances and introduces two new families: the Hesperides and Woods with their subfamilies.

These families are defined through structures accepted by most perfumers, based on a standard association of materials. Thus for the fougère family, the description is FOUGÈRE, *Evocative description, which claims no connection with the odor of fougère and is produced with notes of lavender, oak moss, coumarin, bergamot, geranium, etc.*

I was a member of the SFP's perfume classification committee, and today I wonder about the real utility of such a classification since few people, when reading a definition of this kind, can form any idea of the odor of "fougère," because they are not familiar with the smell of each material and cannot imagine the combination.

When I read the following lines from Jean Giono's *Voyage en Italie,* I am confirmed in my view that classification is impossible: "What bothers me when I speak of a painting is that I find it impossible to describe color; yet that is essential. I can say red, green, yellow, but those words don't help me see anything. It makes everyone think that you have succeeded. But who can claim that he has seen a picture when it has been described to him in words? Describing it with sentiments (which on first view appears better) in the end does nothing more than create further confusion."[6]

As I read this text, the word "sentiment" catches my eye. I read "sentiment" and I hear "scent-I-meant." All classification is subjective, perhaps entirely personal. For this reason, I looked at various types of classification, in particular those of classical music. I learned that for a long time music was classified in terms

---

[6]Jean Giono, *Voyage en Italie*, Paris, Gallimard, "Bibliothèque de la Pléiade," 1995, p. 581.

of structures that are types of construction: ballad, bourrée, canticle, concerto, étude, fugue, minuet, pavane, polka, polonaise, rhapsody, sonata, suite, symphony, waltz, and so forth. Then that in the 1950s many composers rejected these preexisting forms and focused primarily on the sound of the instruments and less on the structure of the music. Nonetheless, we still use classifications when we want to buy a CD, since we choose our music by type: classical, jazz, pop, rock, country, blues, folk, soul, rap, and the like.

However, this classification tells us little about the quality of the music. These days, choices are driven by the names of artists: Norah Jones, Mozart, Brad Meldhau, Charles Trenet, and so on.

In today's perfume classifications, I find that the important information is the date of creation, the names of the perfume and the distributing brands. The date tells you about the development of the fragrance, provided that you can sample it. The brand and product names give you an idea of the creativeness of each firm (see p. 117–119).

Moreover, in their quest for new forms of expression, perfume composers and the market have together produced new structures. The links to earlier perfumes are primarily in the memories of perfumers, as is the odor of the perfumes they use as models. New perfumes have emerged, many have disappeared. Osmothèque is a home for past perfumes.

Structures. Words. Sentiments. None of these approaches is right. What I propose here is a personal typology in which perfumes are defined by their form; in other words the way they are perceived and not by their constituent materials.

Classical, baroque, narrative, figurative, abstract, minimalist, and so forth.

- The Baroques are defined by exaggeration and the space they occupy. The creation of tension through the accentuation of detail.

- The Classicals are perfumes that have become emblems, archetypes, of perfumery.
- The Abstracts are perfumes that do not imitate nature in any way.
- The Figuratives seek to provide a faithful representation of a specific odor.
- The Narratives tell a story, and describe a place or a journey.
- The Minimalists express odor for its own sake, stripped of all sentiment.

Of course, they can all be combined in many different ways.

In this classification, there are no moderns. The word "modern" does not refer to a form of perfume but to a transitory state. The baroque was modern in its time, and it is only a passing of time that has given boundaries and definition to that form of artistic expression.

Creation, which is by definition an open system, resists and even opposes any classification that constitutes a closed system. A new arrangement is a challenge, an adventure.

III. Perfume Criticism

In August 2006, the *New York Times* announced that it had engaged a perfume correspondent. The journalist described his role as follows: "The creation of perfumes is a form of higher artistic expression, equivalent to painting or music. These columns will treat perfume as an art in its own right." He became the first critic of the art of perfume. This news delighted me. It heralded the birth of a new discipline.

For perfume to be recognized as a form of artistic expression, criticism is essential. It is not simply a matter of describing it by listing and unveiling its constituent materials—reading a recipe does not put the taste of the dish on the tongue—but of judging it for its expression, its originality, and its quality, what I call its style. Style separates perfumes from the people who create them. Criticism forces perfume composers to reconsider everything they do, because in a market where all brands are in competition, distinctiveness is more important than novelty, which is only a temporary state. It is this that helps brands to survive.

Perfume criticism first emerged on the web. Starting out as personal blogs, perfume blogs have become significant discussion forums, visited by thousands of people every day. Nowadays, these critics comment on new perfumes. They are free to say what they want, as are web users who also make their own assessments. Whether lovers, gourmets, or connoisseurs, I like their attitudes, their genuine feelings, as long as they remain an independent and critical voice on fragrances and do not become a mouthpiece for brand marketing. I see them as of real benefit to people who like perfumes, to perfumes, and to perfume composers. These comments can only encourage young talent and new approaches to perfume. For a while one can forget the market leaders, which offer no form of critique other than the simple fact that they have pleased a certain percentage of consumers.

Chapter VII

TIME

An hour is not merely an hour, it is a vase filled with perfumes, sounds, projects and climates.

—MARCEL PROUST, *TIME REGAINED*

From the terrace of the Doge's Palace on St Mark's Square in Venice, I contemplate the Clock Tower and its dark blue dial divided into twenty-four hours marked by Roman numerals. Nearby, another dial shows the hours and minutes. It is 10:00 a.m., then 10:05, 10:10, 10:15 . . . While my watch chases hours and minutes, this dial shows not only the time but time itself. And though reason tells me that the clock's time and my watch's are the same, my perception is unconvinced. Because the time intervals are different, I feel that time flows differently. This impression is reinforced by a sense of vertigo as my eye follows the motion of the second hand. But why bring time into it? Because time fashions our thinking, interpenetrates our every moment, molds all the objects we create, and is experienced, represented, or used differently on every continent and by every individual. In India, traditional musical composition is linked with daily and seasonal cycles. In China, painters have never depicted shadows, so that the world they conjure is timeless. Closer to us, the clothing designer Yohji Yamamoto has stated, "My garments have no seasons."

I. Time and Perfumes

Every era is marked by the spirit of the times. This spirit flows freely, irrationally, and is expressed by an ensemble of artistic productions guided by intuitions, instincts, and ideas that are interlinked and resonate together.

I recall conversations with the chef Alain Senderens. His fascination with Japanese food led him to become one of the creators of French *nouvelle cuisine*. He liked to emphasize the influence of presentation and the importance of time, stressing the role of timing marinades in order to achieve optimum balance in the mouth. Precise control cooking times also enabled him to create unique mixtures of hot and cold food. He also talked about the benefits of slow cooking at low temperatures. There is no doubt that his culinary creations are still molded by this culture and by time. By moving from an ingredient-dominated technique to an approach centered on the senses, he has created an identifiable personal aesthetic.

What has this to do with perfume? In the twentieth century, perfumers brilliantly celebrated the materials, the richness, the consistency, the power, the content, and the sources drawn from classical references in their compositions. To showcase this substance-dominated expertise, which would remain the primary model until the late 1970s, perfume formulas were complex; subformulas, mixtures, bases, additions, and doubles were all included in their compositions. Preparations were lengthy, proportions complicated. Preparers could spend a whole day "constructing" a formula. After several months of research, the developed perfume was matured and then macerated in a tank, sometimes for up to six months, in order to facilitate physiochemical reactions.

At the end of that era, the major perfume manufacturers decided to establish olfactory profiles of all the raw materials used in perfumery and studied their activity over time. These technical details might seem anecdotal, but they show that attitudes to time and taste change: in an increasingly competitive market, consumers expected the compositions of their perfumes to be measurable.

Ten years later, focus groups and market testing emerged. Many perfume composers began to take a more technical approach to composition and to assemble so-called "linear" compounds. Perfume had to create the illusion of compactness and express itself continuously without significant variation, with a strong, tight, and lasting presence. Diffusion and retention on the skin became a powerful sales criterion.

This linear composition reminds me of some of the music that emerged at the same time, in which variations in intensity where abandoned so that it could be listened to passively in any environment, unlike classical music or jazz, which play on variations in intensity and therefore require active listening.

Such perfumes only used constituents that retained their primary identity, which varied little over time and could serve to structure the composition. They allowed little room for products of natural origin because their scents change over time, except those that have a consistent aroma like patchouli or sandalwood. Nonetheless, the formulas remained complex since perfume concentrates could be manufactured in less than an hour using automated systems. Maturation became a thing of the past, and the maceration process took place on the store shelf.

Alongside these linear productions, which indeed met the needs of some consumers, another, more conceptual composition has been attracting a different clientele, with perfumes that I call "evolving." In these, the composition can be seen as a harmonious ensemble that changes as it evaporates, with moments of emptiness and fullness, creating constant surprises; style overshadowing matter. The role of the perfumer then becomes to create a succession of olfactory moments. Expression time is no longer experienced as a limit but as a variable that restores the freedom of choice.

The components used, wherever they come from, vary in their aroma over time. Natural in origin, they are complex in composition and difficult to use correctly.

What I am trying to explain as simply as possible is that one mustn't form a definitive opinion based on the formal quality of compositions but treat time as an integral part of any perfume's composition. And the reason for my brief parallel with cooking is that I find in this form of expression perfectly described by Michel Onfray in *La Raison gourmande* (Grasset, 1995) an echo of past and current approaches to perfumery.

II. The Time to Create

I am sorry to admit I have lost the gift of boredom. I write. I read. I garden. I paint. I cook. I vacuum. And although my subsidiary activities are more or less linked to perfumes (apart from vacuuming), I wish to pay tribute to inaction, for taking time is not wasting time. Most of my ideas, my pretexts, have come from chance encounters when reading, when strolling, when idling, moments of unfocused receptivity. It's a matter of grasping the occasion, jotting down a few words, the names of raw materials, and the glimpse of an idea. The time to turn an idea into a creation can vary from a few days to several months. The compositions I have created in a few days seem to have emerged from my memory as if their forms had preexisted. The compositions that took time were created gradually. It has happened that an attempt that did not turn out as I imagined, arising from an unintended combination or a dosage error in one of the components, has shown a new avenue to follow. For this reason, I keep all test samples for several months and let time do its work. I sometimes carry out multiple trials before returning to the perfectible initial attempt to start out on another path. In fact, with this approach, I often have a clearer idea of what I *do not* want and achieve what I do want by elimination.

III. Time to Sense

We all know that perfume unfolds in time and space. At the same time, the very first moment we smell it, we perceive it in its totality. For I only have to remove one so-called background, I prefer the term "distant" component from its composition, to smell the difference. So the distant component is present from the first olfaction. As a perfumer, to ensure that it is present, if I do not know the perfume's formula, I leave a strip of blotter impregnated with the perfume on a postcard clip for forty-eight hours. After this time, many molecules will have evaporated, leaving behind only the most persistent. In metaphorical terms, the bus needs to empty so I can spot the people I know. So perfume has a unique form of expression, in which space and time merge, and also a factor of frustration: the impossibility of concentrating on a perfume, an aroma, for more than a few minutes without becoming saturated, unable to distinguish anything, aware of no more than an olfactory white noise This frustration does not exist with the other senses. While the expression of the molecules is continuous, our nose can only capture moments, intervals of time, perhaps to keep the sense of smell alert. To compensate for this frustration we decode, evaluate, compare intermittently, and work with the memory of the aroma. Wine experts use these properties when assessing wines. They go through a short ritual of looking, smelling, tasting, and then spitting out the wine in order to assess the flavor in its length and its persistence. To smell a perfume is to experience a succession of moments. It is the perfumer's choice to exploit or minimize this effect when they are composing.

IV. Time to Buy

According to the anthropologist Edward T. Hall, every sensory process is linked to a type of distance. To summarize his research, vision is the sense of *public distance*, distance between strangers, sufficient to obtain general information; it corresponds to the distance between teacher and pupils or in a press conference. Hearing is the sense of *social distance*, a distance that is used for communication, that fosters sharing, commercial relations. Touch and taste are the senses of *intimate distance*, that of the glutton, and also the distance of the murmur, the whispered confidence. The sense of smell, which stands between social distance and intimate distance, is called *personal distance*; it is the distance of light conversation, of relations between friends, of shared emotion and experience.

By fostering one type of sensory mode or another, marketing adopts a type of distance from the consumer or the customer, creating a space that cannot be distinguished from the time it takes to buy, which more or less matches the type of product on offer.

Thus, supermarkets prefer the distance of the sense of sight, the quick attention grabber, by creating spaces that are neutral in design, wide, deep, and easy to move around. Brand names and their color codes are clearly defined. The top 10 buys of the week are displayed. Novelties are highlighted. Advertisements show seductive or erotic images, or pictures of celebrities. Everything is visually structured to attract attention. Products are placed at average eye level. Television screens run familiar TV commercials.

The aim is to encourage the impulse buy, to offer instant gratification. Seven minutes is the average time a consumer spends in the fragrance section of a department store.

While specialty stores and boutiques also use brand visuals, their preferred distance is the personal. The space is personalized, and brand names and color codes are clearly defined. In many cases, scent arrays are provided so that customers can sample the perfumes. Individual customer service is offered. You have to wait, take time. The focus is on listening, chatting, advice, and demonstration. Thirty minutes is the average time for a purchase in a specialty store or boutique, long enough to take the time. The aim of this time is to foster personal experience, memorization, and a customer's loyalty to the product.

V. Time at Hermès

In my experience of time at Hermès, I try to be open to the opportunity of the moment and to remain receptive. This state of mind reminds me of a passage in Montaigne's *Essays* where he advises us to live not in the present but "in attunement."

At Hermès, time is articulated around Hermessences, Colognes, and Garden and Novels perfumes. I approach the design of the Hermessence collection with a serenity that I have never experienced. I no longer have any nervous need of winning or conquering "a market." The only customer I have to win over is Hermès. This time is a window for experiments and not a standard schedule imposed by the market, since all the fragrances are sold in specialty stores. So I can take my time, waste time, search, reject, keep, forget, and live my art. I create for myself, in the hope of pleasing others.

There is also much to learn from the time of the Garden. It is in places previously unknown to me that have wrought an emotional shift that circumstances have suggested the choice of each perfume's theme. Fig leaf for *Un Jardin en Méditerranée*, green mango for *Un Jardin sur le Nil*, ginger and water for *Un Jardin après la Mousson*. In each case, the moment of creation was very short, the development time a few months. And if I experienced moments of great anxiety during the first days of the journey for the first two gardens, they were only caused by the fear of not finding the theme and the fear that they might not meet with commercial success. The experience of the first two gardens meant that I could approach the third with peace of mind.

The time of the colognes is similar to the Hermessences in the creative freedom it offers me, but with one significant difference associated with the expression of the product. A moral convention that emerged in the nineteenth century and survives to this day is that eau de cologne should be used for health care, hygiene, for immediate well-being, and devoid of sexuality. These modest apparently harmless products are on the road to transformation since they are underpinned by a pattern of gestures, a ritual, a pleasure that is no longer feigned, and an accepted androgyny.

The design of Novel-perfumes, for wider distribution, is still a source of anxiety, since the market imposes its cycles, which involve replacement and change movement, in fact. Movement fosters novelty. Novelty creates demand. Many perfumes are withdrawn from the shelves before being truly appreciated, which reflects a lack of respect for the customers as well as the perfumers of these fragrances.

In order to keep my distance from the market, I do not create to meet demand; the market is not my benchmark. For a creation to last, for creative freedom, the pace must be chosen, not imposed. In order to make time an ally and allow myself to get lost in my thoughts and my experiments, I have chosen to live away from Paris. As a craftsman and artist, I have a vision of perfume that is expressed by a style in harmony with the world of Hermès. If I need space and light, it is to express my creations in a way that is robust and joyful, vibrant and unburdened.

In a final bid to resist the tense vision we have of time, I would like to end this chapter with a quotation from Jean Giono: "Days [. . .] are not long in shape, that shape of things which have aims: the arrow, the road, the running man. Their shape is round the shape of things that are eternal and static: the sun, the world, God [. . .] Civilized people all [. . .] say that days are long. No, the days are round. We are going towards nothing, precisely because we are going towards everything, and everything is achieved from the moment we have all our senses ready to feel. The days are fruits and our role is to eat them . . . to make them our spiritual flesh and our soul, to live. Living has no other meaning than this."[7]

---

[7]Jean Giono, "Rondeurs des jours," *L'Eau vive*, Gallimard, La Pléïade.

Chapter VIII

MARKETING

You don't even have anything to copy: how can you go wrong?

—WILLIAM FAULKNER

My intention is not to explain marketing as it applies to perfumery, but to situate the role of the composer of perfumes within different forms of marketing.

By way of a reminder, marketing is the set of techniques and analyses used to define, design, promote, and tweak products in order to meet the needs of consumers and to adapt the resulting products to systems of production and distribution.

Historically, marketing emerged in the perfumery industry in the 1970s. In the space of a few years, perfumers moved from commercializing (the word "marketing" was not yet used in France) an elitist product chosen by the company chairman to selling an affordable product defined by the marketing department.

By widening the choice of products, by guaranteeing reliable quality, by offering worldwide distribution and a better return on investment, marketing contributed to the growth of perfume brands and to the transformation of a business into an internationally successful industry.

I. The Marketing of Demand

The objective was to sell perfumes on a global scale. To achieve this, the marketing focus moved away from the selling of products, which were seen as too dependent on conviction and personal choice. To create a global market, the priority shifted to the marketing of demand. Demand marketing operates by continually assessing the needs, habits, and interests of consumers the way they judge products and the pleasure they draw from them. The market is segmented by customer type and products are adapted to specific segments. While this approach can be described as innovative, it is not creative. These products are predesigned to match a specific, targeted consumer profile. The result of this vision of the market is that the brands design products that will please everyone. Choices are guided by tools designed to identify demand and consumer taste: perfume classification, analysis of international markets, trend books (already widespread in the fashion industry), focus groups, and above all, market testing. These approaches have generated perfumes constructed using the technique that I call the *cursor* method. Perfume design is guided by a system of olfactory tick boxes. The criteria are words like "feminine," "masculine," "rare," "rich," "powerful," "light," "elegant," "flowery," "woody," "modern," "classical," "long-lasting," and so forth. The criteria are set by the marketing people and the firm conducting the test. For the composer of perfumes, the potential supplier to the brand, the aim is to produce a perfume that perfectly matches the profile sought by the brand's marketing. The perfume composers choose or reject certain types of odors on the basis of their match with the different criteria, employing this set of *cursors*. This technique has distanced perfumers from the judgement of their own senses and curtailed their creativity. It has provided a foundation for new olfactory conventions, a new conformity. That being said, I find that the overall quality of perfumes has improved. Technically, they have radiance, diffusion, and persistence, and these qualities take months of work. They are good perfumes.

The paradox of the good is that it is identifiable; it doesn't generate surprise. Acceptance and assimilation are immediate. The good is almost always based on commonplaces, on the familiar, and on stereotypes. In addition, this approach, characterized by the pursuit of novelty and success—250 launches in France in 2007—generates a continuous turnover of new perfumes, and consumers constantly shift allegiance.

An awareness of this problem seems to be emerging, and we now see other ways of approaching the fragrance market and, in particular, of attracting customers. The pioneers of these changes are the niche Editions de perfume firms. These are brands like Annick Goutal, L'Artisan Parfumeur, Comme des Garçons, Diptyque, Frédéric Malle, The Different Company, and the like. In my view, the term "niche perfumers" is too restrictive since it defines them solely by their system of distribution—which is primarily their own stores—whereas their commercial approach can be understood through a range of specific criteria and values.

II. Niche Marketing

Since they use little, if any advertising, niche perfume makers focus on the product—the fragrance. The fragrance has to speak for itself and express a strong identity, an olfactory individuality. Great care is taken with the name. The name is the first component in the communication process, and the aim is to generate not consensus but curiosity. The products are mostly sold in small stores, relatively "closed" places where customers are served by attentive, well-trained staff who are totally familiar with the world of perfumes and know the individual story of each fragrance.

A "niche" perfume differs not only in relation to the other perfumes on the market and in its method of distribution but also in the way it reveals its difference. In order to assert its distinctiveness, it must first be judged by professionals. While most commentary and critique comes from journalists in the beauty sector, perfumery professionals, marketing specialists, perfume composers, and judges are the first people to seek out new fragrances; to sample, evaluate, and talk about them; and to use them as reference points. Since distribution is restricted and the products relatively difficult to access, consumers rely on the judgments of the beauty magazines and people trained to present and sell the product. They are also impossible to compare because they are presented in a single place, usually a specialty store, not alongside other brands of perfume.

For a niche perfumer, it is crucial to watch how the customer responds and to establish a relationship with her or him, because the grapevine is very important to the reputation and spread of these products.

For composers of perfumes, whether under commission or free agents, the approach is primarily olfactory—no preadjustment of products for customer segments, no market testing, none of the mythical imagery of advertising, the "plausible stories" Plato speaks of. They are simply unique fragrances, inventions of the mind, which appeal primarily to the olfactory sense.

III. The Marketing of Tomorrow

Inundated with products that are new but devoid of creativity, bored with endlessly similar advertising campaigns where the same model often fronts several brands, customers are treated solely as consumers and fail to find the necessary spark of fantasy, of identity, of pleasure. So they turn to other products, to other sources of fantasy. One marketing solution that the brands can employ to bring back customers is *embodied* perfumery.

The first step in this approach is to understand the style of the brand. The aim is to avoid comparing brand images and to find and establish a distinct identity. To establish a clear vision and to make and keep promises.

In this kind of marketing, the objective is to invent the future of the brand, a vision of what it will offer customers. While a study of the brand can provide a two-hundred-page snapshot of what the customer wants, it cannot provide *the* recipe. The answer lies within those firms where different personalities—artists, designers, decorators—do their creative work, even if this work is peripheral to the brand. Listening to the people who are already building the brand is one way to anticipate the future.

For marketing of this kind, the task is to share the process, the progress of the project, not only with the people who will be responsible for making it work (sales reps and distributors) but with all the staff. It is a collective venture, and perfume is at the heart of the structure. It is not a component within a larger whole but the primary focus. Market testing has no place in this approach, nor does the *brief* in its usual sense. Traditionally, the brief consists of a history of the brand, its positioning vis-à-vis the competition and consumer perception, a concept, images of a woman or a man, a price for the concentrate, and a deadline for proposals.

With the exception of firms that have their own perfume designer, brand marketing entails choosing two or three perfume composers, or perhaps just one, and commissioning him or her or them to complete the project in absolute trust and close collaboration. Competition has no place in the creation of a perfume. It is not about doing better, it is about being unique! The project manager's job is not to manage the creative process but to give the perfume designer the freedom to create. In this process, there is no diffusion of power. The final choice is made by a very small group.

A project, as its name suggests, is a projection of what marketing seeks to achieve, sometimes illustrated by collages and photos. These pictures play an auxiliary role and provide an interface to illustrate the concept. However, while pictures convey information, words are preferable because they require greater thought, a structuring and ordering process. The perfume is built on discussion and interchange. To quote Max Potty, "What you say to me will never be exactly what I understand and vice versa, but from a few significant markers, we agree a form of compromise: an approximate, but nevertheless believable, mutual recognition."[8] This mutual recognition stimulates a dialogue of suggestion that generates desires.

What the composer of perfumes needs to create is the expression of a desire, for it is the desire that we have for an object that makes it beautiful to us, that attracts us.

To put it more concretely, we have all had plans and desires, plans without desire and desires without plans. In the plans for a house, there is the number of rooms, the layout of the spaces, and the number of power sockets. In the desire there is the building, the surroundings, the colors, the textures, and the smells—in fact, oneself.

Since the concept is an abstract and general idea that needs to be given substance, the perfumer composes for himself. Perfume needs real, selected materials to exist. It is the perfumer who creates that existence.

During this journey of the mind, the perfume composer looks to marketing for a critical, intelligent, active, and benign

---

[8]Max Potty, *L'illusion de communiquer*, Paris, L'Harmattan, 2004.

posture. The responsibility is his and he does not rely on outside judgments, which serve only to provide the framework for the project. He opens his mind and reaches a balance. Later on, he will listen to what people say about the creation. "Like" or "don't like" are unimportant. What he primarily looks for is the boundary of rejection.

The success of a perfume is uncertain, it hangs in the balance, where intuition steps outside the frame.

For a perfume to be perceived as different, it must not only assert its difference but also demonstrate it through quality. Here, what matters is the rarity of the odor, the olfactory novelty. It is here that imagination comes in, because the repetitiveness, the ordinariness of a fragrance, comes not from the concept but from the way it is handled. The fact that composers of perfumes use the same natural aromatic ingredients, or the same synthetic products, does not mean that they repeat themselves. It is the way they put those components together that makes the difference. Today, sixty basic ingredients constitute 80 percent of all fragrance formulas.

Only the truly creative disconcerts, offers the unexpected and makes customers think, and generates a shift in attitudes. It widens their perception. It is my belief that this is how brand loyalty is achieved.

Of course, I can create perfumes in the classical manner, or in the baroque, narrative, figurative, abstract, minimalist, and so forth. But above all, I believe that all fragrances should have form, distinction, imagination, generosity, sensuality, and surprise so that perfume is not simply reduced to a product, an object, or a commodity.

IV. To the Marketing People

Let me share a thought with you. Have you noticed in the street, in the cinema, or at the theatre how many perfumes coexist?

I smell *L'Air du Temps, First, N° 5, Eau Sauvage, Shalimar, Opium, Terre d'Hermès, Angel, Eau des Merveilles,* and I am walking through 1947, 1976, 1921, 1966, 1925, 1977, 2006, 1992, 2004. Perfume has something extra that fashion and advertising cannot do: it transports you through time. I don't know of many products that live "outside time" other than works of art. If this is what they would like to achieve, I would like to say to the marketing people: be pioneers! Choose emotion over sensation. Step outside your habitual framework, your systems, and your language. The composition of a perfume, the recipe, and the ingredients can never explain or convey the emotion that a customer feels in smelling a perfume. Share your passions, your desires. This will undoubtedly take more time as we will have to create a common vocabulary to understand each other. It will be more difficult because we will be sharing a part of ourselves. But the result will be innovative, unadulterated, for perfume is not a product that expresses an immediate emotion but a link to the life of the emotions. This link is not verbal but olfactory, fostering encounter, acceptance of the other, and—sometimes—avoidance, which can be a good thing.

Chapter IX

BRINGING THE
PRODUCT TO
THE MARKET

I. The Manufacture of Perfume Concentrate

Apart from Chanel, Hermès, Guerlain, LVMH, and Patou, which have their own in-house perfume makers and create and produce their own perfumes, the perfume concentrate is manufactured by the flavor producers (see Chapter X).

Natural products are purchased at harvest, often in situ. Synthetic products, when not produced by the same company that manufactures the perfume concentrate, are acquired as necessary. All the products bought are tested repeatedly.

The perfume concentrate is made by robots programmed with the perfumer's formula. These machines can weigh anything from a few grams to several tons of product with milligram accuracy and at high speed. Once made, the perfume concentrate is delivered to the perfumery houses, which produce the fragrance and bring it to the market.

II. Perfume Manufacture and Production

The initial step in bringing a perfume to the market is to establish a launch protocol. This document, which is agreed by the firm's marketing, finance and industrial directors, and central management, covers every detail of the manufacture of a product and the costs associated with the different stages.

The manufacturing phases for the different industrial operations are covered by specific, step-by-step procedures called Good Manufacturing Practices or GMP. They must comply with the company's regulatory requirements. These GMP require that a clearly defined, reproducible logical sequence should be implemented at all stages in the manufacture, testing, and finishing of a product in order to guarantee compliance.

The first phase is to inspect and approve all the components of the finished product (bottles, sprays, labels, alcohol, water, perfume concentrate, etc.). These inspections are carried out on the production site to the specifications established by quality control.

All the component management processes are computerized.

The second phase is the manufacture of the fragrance (eau de toilette, eau de parfum, perfume, etc.). This process starts with the manufacture of a small "pilot" batch in order to check and, if necessary, adjust the production process: materials used, blending temperature, duration of maturation and maceration, cooling, and filtration conditions.

After the concentrate has matured for a few days, long enough for the blended odors of the synthetic and natural materials to harmonize, it goes into production. The perfume concentrate is macerated in alcohol for a period of anything from a week to more than a month in order to stabilize the fragrance. Maceration is the outcome of various physiochemical reactions between the perfume components and ethyl alcohol. After this time, the alcohol solution is cooled, filtered, and then stored in nitrogen in stainless steel containers to prevent oxidation.

Once production is complete, a sample of the product is taken and sent to a test laboratory for the batch to be certified. A record is kept of the test result. During the filling operation, each bottle of perfume will be assigned a code corresponding to the production run. This tracking code contains the batch number and the month and year of manufacture.

All these operations are recorded on a computer, and each perfume made has its own file, which is kept for three to five years, depending on the company. Once the production batch has been registered, the unit filling operations begin. Throughout this operation, each production run is monitored. The inspections cover the appearance of the bottle, the cap, the packaging, and the finished product.

III. Safety Regulations

There are numerous safety requirements relating to the distribution of perfumery and cosmetic products.

Historically, in the 1960s the U.S. manufacturers created the Research Institute for Fragrance Material (RIFM). The role of this institute is to do research on the conditions in which raw materials can be used without undesirable effects. These tests are conducted at concentrations ten or more times higher than those of the product itself, in order to give a wide margin of safety. As a self-regulatory mechanism, in 1973 the perfumery industry set up its own body: IFRA—the International Fragrance Association. This body uses the RIFM's data to regulate the use of ingredients and to establish a "code of practice." This information can be accessed on the Web at: www.ifraorg.org.

Since then, perfumery firms have been legally obliged to follow the recommendations of this body. Each raw material comes with an IFRA certificate, and since 1991, all deliveries of scented products have also included a material safety data sheet (MSDS), based on European Directive 91/155/CE, which contains sixteen items of information:

1. the trade name of the product, details of the manufacturer, and supplier;
2. the nature of the product, the CAS[9] number, and EINECS[10] number;
3. identification of the hazards;
4. first aid measures;
5. fire fighting measures;
6. accidental release measures;
7. handling and storage precautions;
8. exposure control and personal protection;
9. physical and chemical properties;
10. product stability and reactivity;
11. toxicological information;
12. ecological information;
13. disposal considerations;
14. transport information;
15. regulatory information (which is covered by further directives);
16. other information.

The MSDS is accompanied by a declaration on potential allergens (so far twenty-six allergens have been identified).

---

[9]Chemical abstract substance.
[10]European inventory of existing commercial chemical substances.

For perfumes, the first legislation on cosmetics in France, the *loi Veil,* was introduced in 1975, followed by a European directive adopted in Brussels in 1976. This directive specifies the obligations both of manufacturers and of member states. It is regularly updated.

Perfumery firms are obliged to comply with the directives. Before a product goes to the market, it must meet a number of conditions:

1. A scented product safety certificate issued by the supplier.
2. Compliance with Cosmetics Directive 76/768 (including regular amendments), which clearly focuses on consumer safety and emphasizes the need for the finished product to be harmless. This directive is incorporated into French law through the Public Health Code.
3. When bringing a product to the market, the firm must complete a declaration with the names and qualities of the people responsible for manufacture, packaging, quality control, and storage.
4. There are strict labeling rules for the finished product, in particular the need for a list of the allergens contained in the scented composition and, if necessary, precautions for use.
5. Batches must be traceable.
6. The manufacturer must guarantee the stability of the end product. If the minimum durability is less than thirty months, the finished product must have a use-by date. Beyond thirty months, the end product must have a period after opening (PAO), i.e., the length of time it can be kept before becoming a health risk.
7. For cosmetic products, the directive sets the microbiological purity criteria, which are assessed through a "challenge test." This test confirms the efficacy of the preservatives in the finished product.

8. It obliges the manufacturer to prove that its product is not harmful. The product's safety certificate is signed by a toxicology expert. Animal testing on finished products is illegal and has been replaced by tests either on cell cultures or with human volunteers. The recommended tests relate to primary skin and eye irritation, in-use tests, phototoxicity, sensitisation, any photosensitivity, depending on the nature of the finished product, and the area of the body it is used on. However, these tests are the sole responsibility of the firm that brings the product to the market. They are therefore not compulsory and not always carried out.

9. In the case of cosmetics that make claims of any kind, the reality of those claims must be demonstrable.

10. The whole formula may need to be supplied to antipoison centers, a process that is compulsory in the event of an accident. There are twelve of these centers in France, located in Angers, Bordeaux, Grenoble, Lille, Lyon, Marseille, Nancy, Paris, Rennes, Rouen, Strasbourg, and Toulouse.

11. Producers must put together a technical pack containing a qualitative and quantitative description of the formula, the operational data, the specifications of the raw materials and of the scented composition, the finished product inspection requirements, the harmlessness data and safety certificate, the microbiological data, the PAO protocol, a photocopy of the declaration to the antipoison centers, and finally a visual of the finished product.

Apart from its obligations under the directive, the company bringing the product to the market must register its products in every country outside Europe.

Asia, Latin America, the Middle East, and Russia require specific procedures, with qualitative and quantitative information, the specifications of the materials and the finished product, and multiple certificates. Certain countries, such as Japan, Saudi Arabia, and Russia, also require special labeling.

Under the directive, as soon as the product comes onto the market, the manufacturer must

1. set up a product safety system to identify any undesirable effects of the finished product and, if necessary, have medical tests carried out;
2. respond to any requests from consumers for information on the finished product (undesirable side-effects, substances classified as carcinogenic, mutagenic or toxic to reproduction, allergens, etc.);
3. provide health authorities or fraud prevention bodies with the technical product files, together with updates, and all documents and procedures that can confirm traceability and manufacturing and monitoring conditions.

In the near future, finished products will no longer be allowed to contain primary ingredients that have been tested on animals and will need to comply with REACH obligations, i.e., the toxicological and eco-toxicological data on each substance or mixture of substances, will need to be checked for reasons of environmental and health protection, and will need to comply with the rules of Good Laboratory Practice or Good Manufacturing Practice.

In addition, the differences in regulations between the three big industrialized zones—Europe, the United States, and Asia—will be phased out with the introduction of a universal system of classification called the *Globally Harmonized System* (GHS). This is expected to result in the establishment of standard labeling.

IV. The Products

"Eau de cologne," "eau de toilette," "eau de parfum," and "perfume" are terms that refer to forms of expression in fragrances and not simply to different concentrations.

Eau de cologne (2 percent of sales in France), which gets its name from the German city of Cologne where the product was first made, was a product used for bodily hygiene and also drank as a panacea for physical discomfort. Since the twentieth century, this product has been associated with both hygiene and comfort, often linked with sporting activity.

In products for women, eau de toilette (50 percent of sales in France) has an Epicurean role and leaves a subtle but detectable trace. Eau de parfum (45 percent of sales in France) leaves a trace that is rich and powerful. Perfume extract (2.5 percent of sales) is the most intense and lasting form of fragrance.

In men's products, eau de toilette represents 90 percent of the market, and aftershave less than 5 percent of sales, and although concentrated eau de toilette—eau de parfum—for men exists, there are few perfume extracts.

V. Concentrations

Although globalization is leading to greater uniformity in taste, when it comes to perfumes, concentration still determines choice. To simplify, Asia and Japan particularly favor fragrances with low concentrations, in order not to mask the odor of the skin. In the United States, they prefer strong concentrations that mask the skin. Northern European tastes resemble the United States while Southern Europeans like their fragrances in moderate concentrations, which enhance the natural odor of the skin.

Depending on where products are made, but also on traditions and habits of use, concentrations vary.

- Eau de cologne contains 2 to 4 percent of concentrated perfume. (Note that the term "cologne" in the United States is equivalent to eau de toilette in Europe.)
- Eau de toilette contains 5 percent to 20 percent of concentrated perfume.
- Eau de Parfum contains between 10 percent and 20 percent of concentrated perfume.
- Perfume proper contains between 15 percent and 35 percent of the concentrate.

Chapter X

THE PLAYERS ON THE WORLD MARKET

I. The Fragrance Industry

The fragrance industry is made up of manufacturers of synthetic and natural base materials, perfume concentrates, and flavor concentrates. The world market in fragrances and flavors was estimated at €15.8 billion in 2008, with France accounting for 15 percent of the total.

Five corporations share 60 percent of the world market.

Givaudan, a Swiss firm. Their headquarters are in Vernier, near Geneva. Givaudan is the world leader, with 18.4 percent of the market. In 2007, it recorded total sales of around €2.830 billion, including the takeover that year of Quest, the Dutch division of the British chemicals group ICI. This is divided between 54 percent flavors and 40 percent fragrances.

www.givaudan.com

Firmenich, a Swiss firm. This family firm was founded in 1895 in Geneva, which remains its headquarters. It is the leader in fine fragrances and holds 12.7 percent of the market with total sales of €1.95 billion in 2007, divided between flavors, perfumes, and ingredients.

www.firmenich.com

IFF or International Flavors and Fragrances, a U.S. firm based in New York. It is one of the world leaders, with 11.5 percent of the market. It recorded total sales of €1.752 billion in 2007, comprising 56 percent fragrances and ingredients, and 44 percent flavors.

www.iff.com

Symrise is a German company, with its headquarters in Holzminden. It holds 9.3 percent of the market. Its total sales figures in 2007 stood at €1.445 billion, 53 percent from fragrances and 47 percent from flavors.

www.symrise.com

Takasago, a Japanese firm with its headquarters in Tokyo. Founded in 1920, Takasago holds 5.6 percent of the world market. Its total sales were around €1.040 billion in 2007, of which 57 percent was in flavors, 21 percent in fragrances, and 22 percent in fine chemicals.

In addition to these leading firms, numerous firms based in Grasse in Southern France are significant players in this sector and also started out as manufacturers of natural raw materials.

II. The Industry in Grasse

Most of the industry in the Grasse region consists of family firms founded in the eighteenth century. They grew and adapted to changes in society, in technology, and in legislation. Although many products are extracted at Grasse, others are imported from production sites in China, North Africa, Indonesia, and the United States. They are processed and adapted to the needs of the perfume composers. Because of its unique fund of expertise, Grasse remains an area that is indispensable to the perfume industry. In 2007, Grasse's fragrance sector earned revenues of €650 million, 70 percent in exports. The Grasse region directly give employment to 3,500 people.

SOME GRASSE FIRMS

Mane. This company, based in Bar-sur-Loup near Grasse, makes compositions of perfumes and flavors and specializes in the production of natural materials. It recorded sales of €333 million in 2007, 43 percent in fragrances, 43 percent in flavors, and 14 percent in raw materials.

www.mane.com

Robertet. A firm founded in 1850 in Grasse, which manufactures compositions of perfume and flavors, specializing in the production of natural raw materials. Group revenues in 2007 were €241 million, including the activity of the company Charabot. These revenues comprise 45 percent flavors, 35 percent fragrances, and 20 percent raw materials.

www.robertet.com

LMR (Laboratoire Monique Remy). Founded in Grasse in 1983, it became a subsidiary of the U.S. firm IFF in 2000. Its sole activity is the manufacture of natural raw materials. It recorded sales of €14.4 million in 2007.

Payan Bertrand. This firm, founded in 1854 in Grasse, is primarily involved in the production of natural raw materials. It recorded sales of €16 million in 2007.

www.payanbertrand.com

III. The Perfumery and Cosmetics Industry

The perfumery and cosmetics industry consists of manufacturers of fragrances, care, and beauty products; makeup products; and health products. On the international scene, most of the perfume and cosmetics brands are American and French. The Japanese brands primarily specialize in cosmetics. The estimated world market stood at €132 billion in 2007. The proportion of perfumes in this total is difficult to evaluate since the figure is not published.

In France, the perfumery and cosmetics industry is a big contributor to the national economy. The French spend an average of €205 per person per year in this sector. World sales in 2007 stood at €16.3 billion, including €6.9 billion for the French market. With a trading surplus of €7.5 billion in 2007, the perfume and cosmetics industry is the French economy's fourth largest exporter. L'Oréal is the world's number 1 cosmetics firm, while the U.S. company Coty is the number 1 in perfumes.

The big players include the following:

LVMH. The Louis Vuitton Moët Hennessy Group sees itself as an ambassador of Western refinement in the art of living. It describes itself as follows: "We want to bring dreams to life through our products and through the culture that they represent, an alliance of tradition and modernity."

LVMH creates and distributes numerous perfume and cosmetics brands, including Christian Dior, Givenchy, Guerlain, Kenzo parfums, Loewe, and Acqua di Parma.

It recorded sales in fragrances and cosmetics of €2.7 billion in 2007.

www.lvmh.com

Chanel. The Chanel Group has, with remarkable consistency over the years, embodied a certain idea of luxury, quality, and French lifestyle with *haute couture,* ready-to-wear, jewellery, accessories, perfumes, and cosmetics. Its sales are estimated at €2.5 billion, primarily generated by fragrances and cosmetics.

www.chanel.com

Hermès. This firm, the ultimate in luxury *à la française,* sees itself not as a fashion firm but as a creator of objects, embodied in its multiple product lines in saddlery, silk, leather work, female fashion, male fashion, shoes, jewellery, tableware, and perfumes. It likes to insist that *"it creates products to last."* The group's fragrance sales in 2008 stood at €1.7 billion, with perfumes accounting for 7 percent of that figure.

www.hermes.com

L'Oréal. This firm is the world number 1 in the cosmetics industry. L'Oréal has always invested in research to maintain the quality, safety, and innovativeness of its products. The group's positioning today is "to add to the beauty of women and men the world over and bring day-to-day answers to their essential need for well-being."

The group creates and distributes numerous perfume brands, including Giorgio Armani, Cacharel, Lancôme, Ralph Lauren, Viktor & Rolf, Guy Laroche, Paloma Picasso, and Diesel.

L'Oréal operates in 130 countries. In 2007, the group recorded sales of €17.1 billion, including an estimated 10 percent in perfumery.

In 2008 L'Oréal acquired Yves Saint Laurent Beauté and Roger & Gallet and the Boucheron, Stella McCartney, Oscar de la Renta, and Ermenegildo Zegna licences.

www.loreal.com

Coty Inc. This U.S. firm is number 1 in perfumery products. Originally a French company, the group draws its inspiration from François Coty's ideas on the potential market for perfumes (see p. 7), provided that they are popularized without losing the idea of luxury.

The group recorded sales of €3.1 billion in 2008.

The Coty Group is divided into two parts:

• *Coty Prestige*, which creates and distributes fragrances and cosmetics from the following brands: Calvin Klein, Cerruti, Chloe, Chopard, Davidoff, House of Phat, Jette Joop, Jil Sander, JOOP!, Kate Moss, Kenneth Cole, Lancaster, Marc Jacobs, Nautica, Nikos, Sarah Jessica Parker, Vera Wang, and Vivienne Westwood.

• *Coty Beauty*, which creates and distributes fragrances and cosmetics from these brands: Adidas, Aspen, Astor, Céline Dion, Chupa Chups, David and Victoria Beckham, Desperate Housewives, Esprit, ex'cla.ma'tion, Isabella Rosselini, Jovan, Kylie Minogue, Miss Sixty, Miss Sporty, Pierre Cardin, Rimmel, Shania Twain, Stetson, and Vanilla Fields.

www.coty.com

Estée Lauder. The U.S. firm Estée Lauder Companies Inc. is one of the top players in the beauty products sector. Its motto is "bringing the best to everyone we touch." The group creates and distributes twenty-eight brands, including Estée Lauder, Aramis, Clinique, Kiton, Donna Karan, Michael Kors, Origine, Prescriptives, Tom Ford, Tommy Hilfiger, Jo Malone, and Missoni.

The group recorded sales of €5.4 billion in 2007.

www.elcompanies.com

Puig Beauty and Fashion. This Spanish firm, founded in 1914 by Puig Antonio, became the Puig Beauty and Fashion

Group in 1996. The perfume business is divided into two divisions, the prestige division and the beauty division. The group is present in 150 countries and creates and distributes numerous brands, including Agua Brave, Carolina Herrera, Comme des Garçons, Prada, Nina Ricci, Paco Rabanne, Gal, Myrurgia, Antonio Puig, and Heno de Pravia. The group recorded sales of €954 million in 2007.

www.puig.com

Procter & Gamble. This U.S. corporation manufactures detergents, soaps, cosmetics, and pharmaceuticals. It is present in 180 countries with three hundred brands. It has revenues of €59.4 billion, including €17.9 billion in the beauty sector.

The group creates and distributes the Baldessarini, Dolce & Gabbana, Dunhill, Hugo Boss, Escada, Giorgio Beverley Hills, Gucci, Jean Patou, Lacoste, Laura Biagiotti, Rochas, and Valentino perfume brands.

www.pg.com

Other significant players include the Anglo-Dutch firm Unilever, which creates and distributes the *Brut* fragrance from Fabergé, and the Japanese firm Shiseido, which is essentially a cosmetics brand but creates and distributes the fragrances Shiseido and Serge Lutens.

IV. Distribution

In France, fragrances are distributed through four types of network:

• *Large-scale distributors,* which generate more than half of total sales in the perfumery and cosmetics industry.

• *Selective Distribution,* which includes some two thousand point of Saks, three-quarters of which belong to the three chains Marionnaud, Sephora, and Nocibé.

• *Sales on Pharmaceutical Advice* which account for around 10 percent of the market.

• *Direct Sales,* primarily driven by two brands: Yves Rocher and Club des Créateurs de Beauté, the second of which belongs to L'Oréal Group and 3 Suisses. They account for 7 percent of the market.

It should be remembered that almost 60 percent of sales in the perfumery and cosmetics industry are in export markets and that there are as many different kinds of distribution processes as there are countries.

Chapter XI

PROTECTION
OF PERFUMES

In the same way as other luxury products, perfumes are particularly vulnerable to counterfeiting and require protection. While names, containers, and packaging can easily be protected in France through the law of trademarks, industrial designs, and geographical indications, protecting a fragrance is more problematical.

I. Protecting Names, Containers, and Packaging

The first stage in the protection of a perfume is to file the name chosen to identify it as a trademark. This process is complex because of the very large number of trademarks already registered in international class 3 (the class that includes fragrances) and the tendency in the industry to adopt evocative names.

The bottle or container is protected by filing a drawing or model, which is protected for a maximum of twenty-five years (four renewable periods of five years). When the bottle is particularly original, distinctive, and identified with the product, it can also be protected by filing a three-dimensional trademark, which is protected for an unlimited period (provided that it is regularly renewed).

Finally, the packaging is usually protected by filing a figurative trademark that shows the whole of the drawing printed on the packaging, and in particular the calligraphy used for the chosen name, the decor, and the colors.

So protecting these different elements poses no particular problems, especially as in the absence of trademark protection, they can also be protected by copyright (principle of cumulative protections) and/or by the rules on unfair competition.

However, this is not true of the fragrance itself.

II. Protection of Fragrances

"Secrecy" is often put forward as the natural way of protecting products since the formulas are carefully stored by the firms and/or composers away from prying eyes.

Nonetheless, for many years, perfumery firms have been looking for other and more effective ways to protect themselves.

1. Protecting Fragrances Through Patents. From a purely legal perspective, there is nothing to stop a fragrance being registered as a patent except the fact that it must be registered in a lasting form (as a full formula and not a perfume sample).

In practice, however, this form of protection seems completely unsuited to the world of perfume since it requires the formula to be published (and therefore the secret to be disclosed) and offers too short a period of protection (twenty years, whereas the lifespan of a perfume can be much longer).

2. Protecting Fragrances Through Trademarks. While there seems to be no specific objection to protecting an odor through trademark law, the laws and precedents pose conditions that stand in the way of registering fragrances as trademarks. In 2002, community jurisprudence, which was initially a pioneer in this field,[11] set very strict protection criteria: an odor, even if represented in a physical medium, in particular a chemical formula, can only be protected under trademark law provided that the graphic representation is "clear, precise, complete in itself, easily accessible, intelligible, lasting, and objective."[12]

For their part, the laws require the trademark to be distinctive. This implies that they should be arbitrarily chosen and should not describe the products or services concerned. Thus, "the smell of fresh cut grass" as a name for tennis balls has been registered as a trademark, but using the odor of a perfume to identify the perfume itself does not seem to be open to such protection.

So trademark law could provide a possible solution for protecting an odor when it is used for sensory marketing (a pen with the scent of orange) but not in the sphere of perfumery.

3. Protecting Fragrances Through Copyright. Works that can be protected under copyright are defined as products of the mind and a nonexhaustive list of them is provided in Intellectual Property Law, which does not mention fragrances.[13]

All the "works" in the above-mentioned list have one thing in common: they are all accessible to the public through sight or hearing. The senses of touch, taste, and smell are all missing from this list. However, it was ruled in 1975[14] that, although the code only mentions works that are perceptible through sight and

---

[11]2nd OHMI Board of Appeal, ruling of February 11, 1999, "Vennoostschap onder Firma Senta Aromatic Marketing."

[12]The European Communities Court of Justice, ruling of December 12, 2002, "Sieckmann."

[13]Article L. 112-1 of the French Intellectual Property Code.

[14]Ruling of the Paris Court of Appeal of July 3, 1975.

hearing, there was nothing in principle to exclude those that are perceptible through the three other senses, provided that they demonstrate originality and carry the "imprint of the personality" of their author.

In a judgement of September 24, 1999 rendered by the Paris *Tribunal de Commerce,* perfume was therefore explicitly recognized for the first time as being a work of the mind: the creation of new perfumes is the outcome of genuine artistic research; it is therefore undeniably a work of the mind.

Since then, different rulings have been delivered in favor of copyright protection for perfumes, in particular a ruling of January 25, 2006 by the fourth chamber of the Paris Court of Appeal, which recalls that Article L. 112-2 of the Intellectual Property Code "does not provide an exhaustive list of works that are eligible under copyright and does not rule out those that are perceptible through the sense of smell. The fixing of the work is not a required criterion of access to protection, provided that its form is perceptible; a fragrance for which an olfactory composition can be determined fulfils this condition. A perfume can therefore constitute a work of the mind eligible for protection under Book 1 of the Intellectual Property Code provided that, in revealing the creative contribution of its author, it is original"; therefore "fragrances are the outcome of a new combination of essences in proportions such that their emanations, by the final olfactory notes that are released, reflect the creative contribution of the designer."

However, in a noted ruling of June 13, 2006, the Court of Cassation seems to cast doubt on this legal precedent by stating that "the fragrance of a perfume, which arises from the simple application of a skill, does not constitute, in the sense of the aforementioned texts [Intellectual Property Code art. L. 112-1 and L. 112-2], the creation of a form of expression that is eligible for the protection of works of the mind under copyright law."

This ruling seems to go against the view of successive judges since 1975 and reduces the composition of fragrances to the simple application of a skill.

It is still too soon to judge the impact of this decision, but it is worth noting that, being rendered by the first civil chamber of the Court of Cassation,[15] it unequivocally states the position of senior magistrates on this question.

This decision is perhaps justified by economic imperatives and the issues that would inevitably be raised by allowing copyright protection for fragrances.

4. Protecting Fragrances Through the Rules of Unfair Competition. Under the law as it currently stands, proceedings under competition law and more generally under civil liability law would seem to be the most effective basis on which to protect fragrances, at least in France.

Several rulings have already sanctioned the production of a fragrance with significant olfactory similarities with that of a competitor,[16] including in cases where the fragrance had not been considered to be sufficiently original and sufficiently marked with the "imprint of the personality" of its author to receive protection under copyright law.[17]

In explaining their decision, the judges considered this type of behavior to be contrary to fair business practice, in that it seeks to profit from the costs incurred by a competitor, for the sole purpose of diverting the customers of the said competitor to a third party and subsequently of causing losses to the said competitor.

---

[15]Disputes about literary and artistic property are referred to the first civil chamber.
[16]Paris and district Court, March 27, 1998; L'Oréal vs. PLD Enterprises.
[17]Paris and district Court, May 25, 2004, Sté L'Oréal et consorts vs. Sté Bellure et Consorts.

When you look at the legal requirements, filing a patent for a perfume formula cannot provide the necessary protection. The patent requires a perfume formula to be filed, which necessarily removes the element of confidentiality. Copyright protection seems to be a more effective solution, especially as there exists a set of analytical techniques that can reveal counterfeits. In what I have already written, I think I have demonstrated that perfume cannot be reduced to a matter of technique or know-how. The fortunate impossibility of defining a work of art confirms perfume's status as a "work of the mind."

PERFUMES AND
THEIR CREATORS

The principal fragrances mentioned in this book follow with the date of their creation and the names of their creators.

L'air du Temps, Nina Ricci, 1948, Francis Fabron.
Amarige, Givenchy, 1991, Dominique Ropion and Jean-Louis Sieuzac.
Aramis, Aramis, 1965, Bernard Chant.
Anaïs Anaïs Cacharel, 1978, Raymond Chaillan and Roger Pellegrino.
Angel, Thierry Mugler, 1992, Olivier Cresp.
Aqva pour Homme, Bulgari, 2004, Jacques Cavallier.
Aromatics Elixir, Clinique, 1972, Bernard Chant.
Arpège, Lanvin, 1927, André Fraysse.
Bandit, Robert Piguet, 1944, Germaine Cellier.
Beautiful, Estée Lauder, 1985, Sophia Grojsman.
Calandre, Paco Rabanne, 1969, Michel Hy.
Calèche, Hermès, 1961, Guy Robert.
Chamade, Guerlain, 1969, Jean-Paul Guerlain.
Charlie, Revlon, 1973, Francis Camail.
Chypre, Coty, 1917, François Coty.
ck one, Calvin Klein, 1994, Alberto Morillas and Harry Fremont.
Cool Water, Davidoff, 1988, Pierre Bourdon.
Déclaration, Cartier, 1992, Jean-Claude Ellena.

Diorissimo, Christian Dior, 1956, Edmond Roudnitska.
Eau de Campagne, Sisley, 1976, Jean-Claude Ellena.
Eau d'Issey, Issey Miyaké, 1992, Jacques Cavallier.
Eau d'Hermès, Hermès, 1951, Edmond Roudnitska.
Eau des Merveilles, Hermès, 2004, Ralph Schwieger and
   Nathalie Feisthauer.
Eau Parfumée au Thé Vert, Bulgari, 1992, Jean-Claude Ellena.
Eau Sauvage, Christian Dior, 1966, Edmond Rounitska.
Eternity for men, Calvin Klein, 1989, Carlos Benaïm.
Femme, Marcel Rochas, 1947, Edmond Roudnitska.
Fidji, Guy Laroche, 1966, Joséphine Catapano.
First, Van Cleef & Arpels, 1976, Jean-Claude Ellena.
Fleur du Mâle, Jean-Paul Gaultier, 2007, Francis Kurkdjian.
Fracas, Robert Piguet, 1948, Germaine Cellier.
Gaultier 2, Jean-Paul Gaultier, 2005, Francis Kurkdjian.
Giorgio, Giorgio Beverly Hills, 1981, non connu.
Habit Rouge, Guerlain, 1965, Jean-Paul Guerlain.
L'Effleurt, 1907, Coty, François Coty.
L'Homme, Yves Saint-Laurent, 2006, Dominique Ropion,
   Pierre Wargnye and Anne Flipo.
L'Instant, Guerlain, 2004, Maurice Roucel.
L, Lolita Lempicka, 2006, Maurice Roucel.
Le Mâle, Jean-Paul Gaultier, 1995, Francis Kurkdjian.
L'Heure Bleue, Guerlain, 1912, Jacques Guerlain.
Insolence, Guerlain, 2006, Maurice Roucel.
Kelly Calèche, Hermès, 2007, Jean-Claude Ellena.
Kenzo pour Homme, Kenzo, 1991, Christian Mathieu.
Kouros, Yves Saint-Laurent, 1981, Pierre Bourdon
J'adore, Christian Dior, 1999, Calice Becker.
Jazz, Yves Saint-Laurent, 1988, Jean-Francois Latty.
Mania, Giorgio Armani, 2000, Jacques Cavallier.
Miracle, Lancôme, 2001, Alberto Morillas and Harry Fremont.

Mitsouko, Guerlain, 1919, Jacques Guerlain.

Miss Dior, Christian Dior, 1947, Jean Carles.

Miss Dior Chérie, Christian Dior, 2006, Christine Nagel.

Muguet du Bonheur, Caron, 1952, Michel Morsetti.

Must, Cartier, 1981, Jean-Jacques Diener.

N° 5, Chanel, 1921, Ernest Beaux.

N° 19, Chanel, 1970, Henri Robert.

Organza, Givenchy, 1996, Sophie Labbé.

Opium, Yves Saint-Laurent, 1977, Jean-Louis Sieuzac.

Pleasures, Estée Lauder, 1995.

Polo, Raph Lauren, 1978, Carlos Benaïm.

Poison, Christian Dior, 1985, Édouard Fléchier.

Rive Gauche, Yves Saint-Laurent, 1970, Michel Hy and
    Jacques Polge.

Shalimar, Guerlain, 1925, Jacques Guerlain.

Tabac Blond, Caron, 1919, Ernest Daltroff.

Tabu, Dana, 1932, Jean Carles.

Terre d'Hermès, Hermès, 2006, Jean-Claude Ellena.

Trésor, Lancôme, 1990, Sophia Grojsman.

Un Jardin en Méditerranée, Hermès, 2003, Jean-Claude Ellena.

Un Jardin sur le Nil, Hermès, 2005, Jean-Claude Ellena.

Vent Vert, 1947, Pierre Balmain, Germaine Cellier.

Vétiver, Guerlain, 1959, Jean-Paul Guerlain.

White Linen, Estée Lauder, 1978, Sophia Grojsman.

XS pour Homme, Paco Rabanne, 1993, Gérard Anthony.

Youth-Dew, Estée Lauder, 1953, Joséphine Catapano.

GLOSSARY

Absolute: Product obtained from cold extraction of the soluble parts of the concrete.

Accord: Olfactory outcome of a minimum combination of two fragrant materials.

Aldehyde: This word refers to a chemical function and certain synthetic substances with an intense odor. Aldehydes have been used in perfumery since 1905.

Amber: The word "amber" refers to a base, a combination of a few substances, characterized by the presence of vanillin and labdanum. This accord is present in amber perfumes that are sometimes called orientals.

Ambergris: Pathological secretion from the intestines of the sperm whale. The whale evacuates the substance, which floats away and is collected on the seashore. It is rarely used.

Archetype: A perfume that is judged for its characteristic properties. Perfection in its category. It forms the nucleus of perfumes that share a family resemblance and olfactory similarities.

Balsam: Plant exudation product that can be used directly in the composition of a perfume.

Base: Harmonious mixture of a few substances often around a new synthetic molecule.

Chromatography: Analytical technique used to discover, identify, and dose the components of a raw material or perfume.

Chypre: Name given to a category of perfumes. A chypre accord is obtained by combining oak moss, labdanum, and patchouli.

Concrete: Product obtained by extraction of fresh plant materials (flowers, leaves, lichens, seeds, wood, etc.) by means of a volatile solvent.

Eau de cologne: Name taken from the German town Köln (Cologne in French). This is a perfume composed essentially of citrus highly diluted in 70° of ethyl alcohol.

Eau de toilette: Fragrance composed of ethyl alcohol, water, a perfume concentrate, and sometimes a colorant. The concentration of an eau de toilette is an aesthetic choice.

Essence: Product obtained by cold expression of citrus peel.

Essential oil: Product obtained by distilling fresh or dried plants with water vapor.

Extract: Perfume in its most concentrated form.

Headspace: Analytic technique used primarily in situ to capture the odor released by plants: flowers, fruit, and so forth. The substances captured in an absorbent filter are analyzed and identified in the laboratory by chromatography and mass spectrometry then reconstructed.

Fougère: Fictional name given to a category of perfumes. A fougère accord is obtained by combining tree moss, lavender, and coumarin.

Infusion: Alcoholic product containing a diluted natural or synthetic base material macerated for several months.

Maceration: Time required for a perfume to become olfactively stable. Maceration is the outcome of various physiochemical reactions between the perfume components and ethyl alcohol.

Maturation: Time required for a perfume concentrate, a mixture of synthetic and natural materials, to harmonize olfactively.

Medium: Substance used to dilute a perfume concentrate (alcohol, gas, detergent, soap, etc.).

Musk: Very long-lasting synthetic product. Musk is also a substance of animal origin, but it is rarely used in this form.

Resinoid: Product obtained by extracting balsams in ethyl alcohol then evaporating off the alcohol.

Smelling paper (blotter): Strip of blotting paper used to smell materials and perfumes.

Solid-phase microextraction (SPME): A more portable analytical technique than *headspace* as it uses a syringe fitted with a fiber impregnated with an ad hoc medium, which captures and concentrates the volatile compounds to be analyzed.

SUGGESTED READING

Below are a few works where the reader will be able to learn more.

HISTORY

La Parfumerie française et l'art dans la présentation, Paris, 1925.

Annick Le Guérer, *Le parfum, des origines à nos jours*, Paris, Odile Jacob, 2005.

PERFUMERS

Edmond Roudnitska, *L'esthétique en question*, Paris, PUF, 1977.

Elisabeth Barillé, *Coty*, Paris, Éd. Assouline, 1995.

SCIENCE AND TECHNOLOGY

N. Neuner-Jehle, F. Etzweiler, *The Measuring of Odors* by N. Neuner-Jehle and F. Etzweiler, *Perfumes: Art, Science and Technology*, London, Elsevier Applied Science, 1991.

André Holley, *Éloge de l'Odorat*, Paris, Odile Jacob, 1999.

PERFUMED PLANTS

Antonin Rollet, *Plantes à Parfums*, Paris, Éd. CME, 1998.

THANKS

I am self-taught and have become who I am through encounters with people and individuals and, of course, with their work. So I start by thanking my family and my children then the friends—musicians, painters, writers, artists, philosophers, photographs, scientists, lawyers—whom I have met, read, or simply listened to.

And my thanks go too, of course, to the House of Hermès, a place of craftsmen and artists.